the
good
mother
myth

the
good
mother
myth

REDEFINING MOTHERHOOD TO FIT REALITY

EDITED BY **AVITAL NORMAN NATHMAN**
FOREWORD BY **CHRISTY TURLINGTON BURNS**

SEAL

The Good Mother Myth
Seal Press
Copyright © 2014 Avital Norman Nathman
Published by Seal Press
A Member of the Perseus Books Group
1700 Fourth Street
Berkeley, CA 94710
www.sealpress.com

Sarah Emily Tuttle-Singer's essay "No More Fakebook" is a reprint from Kveller.com. Reprinted courtesy of Kveller.com, where it originally appeared on February 25, 2013.

Jennifer Baumgardner's essay "All the Single Ladies" originally appeared in F'em! © 2011 by Jennifer Baumgardner, published by Seal Press.

    Library of Congress Cataloging-in-Publication Data

Good mother myth : redefining motherhood to fit reality / edited by Avital Norman Nathman.
    pages cm
Includes bibliographical references and index.
ISBN 978-1-58005-502-4
1. Motherhood. 2. Parenthood. I. Nathman, Avital Norman.
HQ759.G5876 2013
306.874'3--dc23

                        2013034424

Cover design by Faceout Studio, Tim Green
Interior design by Amber Pirker
Printed in the United States
Distributed by Publishers Group West

FOR MARC AND ELIJAH

Without whom I wouldn't have ever been a mother . . .
let alone had a chance at being a "good" one

CONTENTS

MAMA, DON'T FAIL ME NOW . . .

IN THE MAMA TRENCHES

FOREWORD /
CHRISTY TURLINGTON BURNS

S AN ADVOCATE for global maternal health, I think about moms and our quality of life a lot. I founded Every Mother Counts with a goal to make pregnancy and childbirth safer for all moms following the childbirth-related complication I experienced after delivering my daughter in 2003. Once I learned that hundreds of thousands of girls and women die every year from preventable, birth-related complications, I decided to take action.

What I have learned over the years since becoming a mom is that whether you live in a society where motherhood is celebrated, or in one where it is simply assumed, most of us could better fulfill our roles as mothers if we had more support from one another. While Every Mother Counts's mission is to reduce preventable deaths at birth, I have become increasingly concerned with the full spectrum of issues that are harmful to the lives of mothers, especially those that reduce or demean our roles in society—not just as mothers, but as women.

In my own life, I've come to appreciate the challenge of integrating my roles as a woman, a professional, and as a mother, because in making the attempt as women to be fully human, we let our children grow up seeing our motherhood not as one of total self-sacrifice, but one where we take care of ourselves, and in doing so, take better care of others.

While in the Western World, we have some of the greatest rights and privileges as women and mothers than anywhere else in the world, we yet have an insidious burden working against our empowerment and freedom. It is the deeply entrenched ideal of the Good Mother. It's a myth that is largely predicated on patriarchal constructs, one that creates false standards that sets women up for failure, not success, and for judgment instead of support. It is an attempt to disempower the experience of motherhood. It tells us we are not worthy of our power to create, and that we must conform to narrow ideals of what makes a mother "good." It robs us of our capacity to mother to the best of our own ability—individually, with varying sensibilities and contexts— and makes us doubt not just ourselves but other women—whether they have children or not! Sadly, the Good Mother Myth functions as a check and balance against our ability to create a rich and varied community of women who are valued for their freedom to mother in a way that works for them, not in a way that conforms to narrow ideals of "perfection." It's no wonder so many women struggle with their sense of value and self-worth, especially evolving mothers here and abroad who are just now discovering greater freedoms than being simply a conduit for bringing children into the world.

At this point in time, the possibility and importance of connecting, empowering, supporting, and *accepting* each other as women and mothers at every point along the mothering spectrum is crucial. To evolve as humans we must let go of behaviors and attitudes that hold the whole of humanity back. As mothers, we must do the same. The Good Mother Myth is harmful in its earnestness to define what motherhood means at the expense of women as individuals and as a community. It *divides* us, and what divides us makes us less powerful.

That's why the essays inside this book are so important. They are the collective consciousness of ever-evolving women who share the experience known as motherhood. At times poignant, challenging, funny, and subversive, the essays together represent the spectrum of women who have abandoned or flouted the narrow confines of the Good Mother Myth, often revealing individual perspectives that are also universal.

Together, our stories weave a fabric of motherhood that is textured and intricate and sometimes even flawed, but in its entirety, is also beautiful and more powerful than most of us realize.

INTRODUCTION

hER KIDS HAVE ALWAYS slept through the night, and even if they don't, she still manages to *look* like she has had eight hours of uninterrupted sleep. There is always a well-balanced, home-cooked meal on her dinner table. She holds down a fulfilling job while still finding time to join the PTA, run the school's book fair, and attend every soccer game. Her house is absolutely spotless, and if it's not, she can effortlessly laugh it off. She has the energy and desire for a happy and adventurous sex life, and her partner is always satisfied. She is crafty, creative, and embodies the perfect blend of modern woman and hipster housewife. She is usually white, middle to upper class, heterosexual, married, and neither too young nor too old.

But above all . . . she's a myth.

The myth of the "good mother" is one continuously embedded in our lives, passed down from generation to generation, shape-shifting to fit the nuances of culture and society but always imbued with a fabled ideal of what constitutes the perfect mother. Today she starts even earlier, manifesting herself as the "good pregnant woman" and the "good birther," piling on multiple layers to this already formidable archetype.

This Good Mother has been cemented into our society through television, movies, and most recently, via the Internet, where social networking sites like Facebook, Pinterest, Twitter, and the explosion of "mommy blogs" feed us images and ideas of perfection at a rate faster than ever before. And we are not just eating it up, we are measuring our own motherhood against it all. But a good chunk of these impressions are just that: dressed up or watered down versions of reality. In other words, all of these perfectly executed nurseries, beautifully decorated birthday cakes, Martha Stewart-quality holiday meals and hyper-organized playdates are feeding into the ever-growing myth.

Motherhood as a topic du jour has also remained a staple of the news media, providing endless fodder for websites, magazines, daytime talk shows, and political debate. The majority of these stories hardly begin to scratch the surface of what motherhood really looks like. Instead, cute and quippy sound bytes end up sanitizing the concept of motherhood, or they go to the other end of the spectrum, fostering a manufactured culture of conflict and judgment.

As the myth grows, so too do the negative consequences of its saturation in our lives. The so-called Mommy Wars, mother's guilt, peer judgment, mental illness, and postpartum depression have all been caused or exacerbated by the unrealistic expectations promoted by the Good Mother Myth.

It's insidious on a systemic level as well, because as we focus so much energy on the red herring of perfection, we are forgetting the institutional problems, such as how far the United States is behind other countries in many ways: from reproductive freedom and equal pay to not having mandated, paid parental leave, not to mention dealing with a corporate culture rampant with sexism that does not favor working mothers.

I remember the first time I truly absorbed how detrimental the Good Mother Myth really was. My son was only four weeks old, and we were alone together for the first time. My husband had gone back to work, the endless parade of friends and family had slowed down, and an eerie sense of calm and quiet had spread throughout our home. I had just folded a load of laundry, and found myself sitting on the couch, my son happily nursing away in my arms, wondering . . . *what now?*

I felt like I should have had some idea of what to do, but I was drawing a blank. I had no urge to clean the house, cook, or even sing to my son. I didn't feel sad or upset. I simply didn't feel much of *anything*. It was that overwhelming sense of apathy that scared me. *I should be enjoying this,* I thought. Why was I not reveling in this domestic bliss, I wondered. I sat there, a little spaced out, until I heard somebody at the door. Eager for a little adult interaction, I placed my son on the couch and ran to the front door to greet what turned out to be a UPS delivery man.

Only seconds later I heard a wail that pierced through my heart and jump-started all those feelings that had, only moments earlier, gone numb. In the few seconds that I had been at the front door and signed for my package, my son had somehow rolled off the couch and onto the hardwood floor. I quickly shut the door, rushed to him, inspected him for any bleeding and bruising (there was none), and desperately tried to stick my breast into his wailing mouth. As he finally began to nurse, I took a deep breath, my panic subsiding along with his cries.

I spent the rest of that afternoon alternating between falling apart into a sobbing mess and mentally berating myself:

A good mother would never feel apathy toward her obviously privileged life. A good mother would have known not to leave her baby on the couch unattended. A good mother would not be sitting on the floor, still sobbing, when her husband comes home for dinner that is obviously still not prepared.

Eventually I got over myself. Of course, that was only the first of many future encounters with how my story wasn't falling in line with that of the Good Mother's. She would cross my path many times throughout my son's infancy and toddlerhood. We still go head-to-head in battle now. But the one thing I found was that the moment I shared my story with another parent, no matter how ashamed and nervous that made me, I could breathe a little easier. And so, I began seeking out more stories of mothers dealing with realities that weren't reflected in much of the media.

I was surprised to find that many other women were just as frustrated and annoyed with this myth as I was. They felt as if they were being held up to unrealistic and arbitrary standards. Who created this measuring stick for what is good enough and then proceeded to spread it as gospel? The more I spoke with other moms, the more I realized that the narrative surrounding the Good Mother will only change if we share the realities of *our* lives and deconstruct this myth, which for too long has been hijacking the hearts, minds, and attention of women across every economic, social, and racial background—some more than others.

The women who are sharing their stories here have also had enough of this so-called Good Mother. Together we're cutting the myth of her existence off at the knees. Within this anthology you will find an array of *real* stories of motherhood—the beautiful and funny, messy and heartbreaking. They are at times full of wit and warmth, celebrating our quirky imperfections, while at other times, the poignancy, pain, and sacrifice will wrestle your heart to the ground and fill you with compassion. Raw, diverse, candid, and unapologetic, together these stories aim for a collective goal: to change the narrative of what it means to be a good mother and retire the tired tropes of motherhood that are consistently fed to us in our day to day lives.

But make no mistake, the women who have lent their voices to this collection are *good* mothers. Their stories and their lives reflect what it means to mother outside stereotype and expectation. From professors to porn directors, musicians to massage therapists—black and white, lesbian and straight—these are women writers, well-known and new, who are saying "the hell with it" and "no" and "fuck yes!" and "I'm not happy" and "bring it on!" They write of surprise pregnancies and adoption, sexuality and silent pain, bad breath and poor cooking skills, teenage motherhood and even miscarriage. There are stories of AWOL dads and dads who become mothers, working moms and single moms, as well as moms of multiples. One mom laments the end of her child's cuteness while another admits to sanitizing daily life via social media.

And while the women here are as varied as the spectrum of their stories, they share one thing in common: Their personal landscape of motherhood is guided by the geography of their individual hearts, and by walking their own paths they are creating new definitions of what it means to be a good mother. As you delve into these stories, I invite you to think about your own motherhood journey and what has helped shape it. Read these stories, find yourself within these pages, and join us as we redefine the myth of motherhood to fit reality.

PART I

MAMA, DON'T FAIL ME NOW . . .

ICHABOD'S GHOST /
ABBY SHER

THE FIRST TIME I DROPPED my daughter Sonya on her head from a great height, she was about eight months old. We were staying overnight at my uncle's cabin in the backwoods of Connecticut. There was a plaque by the front door of the house that read: 1789, ICHABOD STODDARD. My cousins still swore Ichabod's ghost visited them, flickering the lights or moving the little pie pieces during games of Trivial Pursuit. Ichabod had built the house with thick slabs of wood and wasn't too keen on making sure the nails sat flush in the floorboards. My uncle hadn't done much in the way of home improvement either. But I digress, and really, I can't blame any of this on Ichabod or my Uncle Murray.

I tucked Sonya in securely next to me on the four-poster bed of Ichabod's attic loft—a good three feet off the ground. And by "tucked in securely," I mean nestled in a divot of the lumpy mattress. You'd think I would have put her on the side closest to the wall instead of the floor, but I wanted her to have more room, which was thoughtful/thoughtless, depending on your point of view. Either way, somewhere between Trivial Pursuit and dawn, in the inkiest black of night, I heard a crash, followed by this very distinct sound:

Waaaaaaaaaaah!

It took a few moments for me to swim up from unconsciousness, and then my first stroke of brilliance was, *Don't turn on the lights, that will wake her up!* Duh. I groped on the floor and scooped her up, poking and petting to make sure there was no blood. Kissing her tears, chanting, "You're okay, you're okay," as much to convince myself as her. The rest of the house was still silent with slumber. My husband was away on work, my cousins were busy dreaming of sugarplum Ichabod fairies, and the woods outside soaked up any chirp or growl, and any sign of civilization for miles. I was supposedly the one in charge here. As we both grew sleepy in the rocking chair, I wondered, *Aren't there things I should check in cases of head trauma? I shouldn't let her sleep if she has a concussion, right?*

Next thing I knew, the sun was tickling us through the attic window and Sonya was babbling next to me. I checked her eyes—alert and bright, though maybe a little less trusting. "Sorry about that," I mumbled, and she pulled down my shirt to take a drink. When we went home the next day, I relayed the story to my husband and declared it was time to stop co-sleeping.

The next time I dropped my daughter Sonya on her head from a great height, we were in Upstate New York. She was two by then (no thanks to me) and had just overcome her fear of the water. We were visiting my father-in-law near a lake. Despite the rolling thunder, I insisted we should go in the water for a romp. The lifeguards only allowed us to dip our toes until they could clock in an hour without any signs of storm. When the "all clear" whistle blew, sandy butts ran in from all sides. It was packed, buoy-to-buoy. The perfect place to experiment with Sonya's new aquatic skills. Or so I thought.

In my defense, I didn't drop her so much as just let her go.

"No!" she yelped.

"You can do it. I'm right here." I started backing away from her, arms still stretched toward her, just a few inches between us really.

"Mama!" she insisted. This was how she was supposed to learn, right? Besides, it was only about three feet deep.

"You got it," I coaxed, backing up again. Only she didn't. She started sinking. That one sounded more like a whoosh, and then . . .

Waaaaaaaaaaah!

Another bather next to me swooped an arm out and caught her as she sputtered and coughed. I rushed back through the water, creating a tiny tsunami in front of me.

"Sorry," I said sheepishly to the man holding my child. "Sorry," I whispered into Sonya's neck as she sobbed.

"I didn't got it," Sonya moaned. "And you left me."

"You're okay, you're okay," I said for the umpteenth time in two years. I got us both wrapped up in sandy towels and handed her to my husband for safekeeping. "Mama made a mistake," I muttered shamefully. By now the biggest question I had was *who let me be a mom, and is there a way to rethink that decision?*

The third time I dropped my daughter Sonya on her head from a great height was definitely the worst. She was three, and also a big sister by then (so much for rethinking that motherhood decision). I picked Sonya up from preschool with her friend Bella. My son, Zev, was in the stroller, Bella was holding on to the side, and Sonya was riding on my shoulders—a favorite treat of hers. Did I mention it was pouring rain and I was also trying to keep an umbrella over the three of us?

We made it across the busiest street in Brooklyn and were just outside our apartment gate. I paused to take Sonya off my shoulders so we could fit through the door. Only I didn't say that plan out loud.

I just sort of hunched forward, and she compensated by leaning back. Then I leaned back and she went back. And back. And back. Until . . .

The sound of a small skull hitting asphalt is beyond bone chilling. And before she could even let out a *Waaaaaaaaaaah!* there were several horrifying moments of her silently searching the sky.

"You're okay, you're okay. Fuck shit, okay, you're okay." I picked Sonya up and clutched her to my chest, pushing Bella and the stroller through the doors as we all whimpered. Blessedly my husband was close by, as was Bella's mom, and we dropped Bella off and drove to the ER within the hour. The whole ride there Sonya was saying how sleepy she was, and I frantically shoved lollipops in her mouth and made up games to play like, "Let's name our favorite color between one and ten."

The ER staff was kind and nonjudgmental as I told the whole story, though one nurse asked me how tall I was and I'd never felt so guilty as when I had to answer, "Five foot eight."

We got to see lots of other pediatric patients with dripping wounds and TB coughs. Each hour we waited, Sonya perked up, playing with the building blocks that had obviously been sucked and chewed on by emergency-level sick kids before her. Zev was pawing at the blood pressure machines and looking for new floor tiles to lick. I will be forever grateful to a man named Dr. Octavio, who finally swooped in, asked Sonya to name all the numbers on the ceiling (a talent I didn't know she had), looked into her eyes, checked her pulse, and then sent us home with balloon animals made out of surgical gloves.

It took me a week to stop rereading the list of concussion signs that Dr. O mentioned. And another year of talk-therapy to name all the reasons why I thought I should give up on motherhood and run away before I did permanent damage.

The one who actually calmed me down and reassured me that I wasn't the worst mother on earth was Sonya herself.

A few weeks ago, while Zev was napping, Sonya and I had some alone time painting. She asked me to draw a rainbow for her on the edge of her paper, which I did. I'll admit it wasn't my best work. The lines sort of ran together and I wasn't careful about rinsing the brushes between colors.

"What do you think?" I asked, after the final swipe of purple.

Sonya squinted at the page before answering. "It's . . . well . . ." Then she picked up her favorite dolly from her art table and said, "Sorry, Mom, Bippy and I need to have a talk for a minute."

She walked Bippy a few feet away and told her in a stage whisper, "I know. I know. But that's not a nice thing to say. I think Mom's doing a great job."

In that moment, I wanted to laugh and cry and hold my beautiful daughter so tight with love.

Instead I bit my lip and said, "Yeah, Bippy. Sorry. But at least I'm learning."

MY LITTLE EARLY PERFECT /
STEPHANIE KALOI

tWO MONTHS BEFORE MY SON was due, I woke in the middle of the night with pangs in my stomach. Despite my overwhelming craving for carrots, these weren't hunger pains. I figured they were simply the Braxton Hicks contractions I'd so often heard about. *No biggie*, I thought, and went back to what was more pressing: getting myself some carrots.

I got out of bed, sat on the floor in front of the fridge, and munched while my husband videotaped my seemingly stereotypical pregnant woman moment. This led into yet another "What will life be like once the baby is here?" conversation—this time about the middle-of-the-night breastfeeding sessions I knew would be in the not-so-distant future. I had a cozy rocker, a big bed, and an accommodating husband. Nighttime feedings? No biggie. I was looking forward to the snuggling. As I munched and chatted while my husband taped, the pangs grew slightly more intense, but they were still manageable. Nothing was even approaching scary, so I washed down the carrots with a glass of milk and went back to bed.

You can imagine my surprise when I moseyed into my midwife's office the next morning, mentioned the pangs at the end of the appointment, and was promptly tested for preterm labor. I went about my day, met my husband for lunch, and the pangs grew stronger. I called the hospital to check in on my tests and was told that I needed to return—immediately. The results indicated I was at risk for going into early labor. Oddly enough, my initial feeling was one of excitement. This was soon quickly replaced by worry and mild panic, but I had a high level of trust in my midwife and the hospital I was planning to deliver at, and for a brief moment, the idea of meeting my baby that very day was an exciting one—before I reminded myself that we were way ahead of schedule.

When my husband and I arrived at the labor and delivery wing, we were both giggling nervously—the nurse at triage looked skeptical when I told her I was asked to come in because I was at risk for preterm labor. Then another wave hit, and I knelt down in the middle of the hallway. Things started to get a little more serious at this point, and I started to realize what my body was preparing to surrender itself to. All of a sudden, this was *not* fun.

The doctors and nurses attempted to stop or stall my labor, to no avail. There was no shred of excitement left in me. I was terrified and confused, asking each nurse I met what was happening to me. I was reassured at every turn: "We're taking care of you" and "We'll keep your baby safe." I couldn't fully comprehend what was happening, and when I found myself being wheeled into a delivery room and being set up for birthing, I still thought the labor would be stopped. It had to be! And then the doctor walked in and announced that I was dilated five centimeters.

Game on.

Up until it ended abruptly, my pregnancy was completely blissful. I had next to no morning sickness, continued to ride my bicycle up until my thirtieth week, when my balance got too wonky, and had developed only one tiny stretch mark. I couldn't seem to find a job as an obviously pregnant woman, so I spent most of my time roaming the streets and dog parks of Portland with our adopted mutt and satisfying my near-constant craving for wontons, which I ate almost as frequently as carrots. Life was great, and I reveled in the experience of growing this little human. In fact, I'd go so far as to say it was totally awesome to be pregnant. It was everything I expected and more.

But everything about the moment I became a mother—and by this I mean the moment I physically *held* my child in my arms—was the opposite of what I'd expected.

Until that day, I never knew that an experience could be simultaneously extraordinary and heart-wrenching—how one moment could shake your soul and rattle your insides and give you terrible dreams at night, while also inspiring you to gush with delirious happiness about how you'd done it: You had entered into that forever life-changing realm that is motherhood. Before I became one, parenthood seemed mysterious to me. But then, as they say, it all clicked the moment I met him.

As my body took over and my personal will was taken over by primitive reflexes, I realized I couldn't stop or alter anything that was happening to me. My son was going to be born that day. His birth wasn't going to happen the way we thought it would, but *it was still happening.* I had one chance to really cherish and remember my son's birth—the moment I was also born as a parent—and this was it.

So I did.

I grabbed my husband's hand and pushed. I pushed, again and again. I yelled, I fought, and shortly thereafter I gave birth to the most incredible little person I had ever seen in my life. But there was no moment of first touch—my hand grazed his chest as they placed him on the NICU table and whisked him away—no cooing or gasping in awe over this adorable little human that my husband and I, weary and battle-worn as we were, had made. There wasn't a chance to try breastfeeding right away or to connect skin-to-skin. One second he was in my body, the next he was wheeled away to be assessed.

And that was it. I had spent the months leading up to our son's birth daydreaming about holding a tiny wrinkly creature, happily whispering sweet nothings and singing Beatles songs in his ear, smiling and loving everything we had done. And I had looked forward to establishing a strong breastfeeding connection and having that quintessential bonding moment.

Instead, the only thing I had to cling to was the area of my hand that had touched his body for that brief moment. I didn't even know if the spot of blood left there in passing was mine or his. I was wheeled into my room, which I would be sharing with a new mother and her baby. Every time her child cooed or cried, my body ached for my own child two floors up and my breasts responded in kind. As if by magic, a nurse came into my side of the room and introduced me to my new best friend: the hospital-grade breast pump I would be using to help feed my child. I immediately began pumping, relieved and happy that I could at least deliver a few drops of precious colostrum to my new son when I took my first trip to see him a few hours later.

I was ecstatic upon meeting my son in the NICU for the first time. Everyone was surprised—many parents are overwhelmed by the sterile environment, filled with monitors and the constant sounds of machines beeping. My husband had visited our son as soon as he knew I was ok, and had spent most of the time crying at his bedside. I was euphoric: NICU or not, this was my baby and I was ready to be his mom.

I was also proud: Our son was larger than average for his gestational age, and from the beginning he was able to breathe without assistance. This meant I could hold him skin to skin on my chest, as the nurse poured my pumped milk into his feeding tube. Even my husband got a turn. It was the next best thing to actual breastfeeding, and he was was always happiest when we held him skin to skin.

A month of back-and-forth NICU visits followed. I pumped

religiously, setting alarms for exactly the times my son's nurses said he needed to be fed. I would wake up each day at 6:00AM, pack my bags of "liquid gold" in a tiny cooler, and set off on my bus ride. I spent hours there with our son (my husband always joined when he wasn't at work), as many as twelve to fourteen hours at a time. Our son was quickly able to receive breast milk by bottle, and by the second week of his life I was encouraged to attempt to feed him at breast. I was nervous and excited, dreading the possibility that he would resist. Instead, he took to it like a champ, and we never experienced any breastfeeding problems from that initial feeding until he self-weaned at fifteen months.

The relationship I developed with the breast pump saved me from what would have otherwise been a miserable month of existence filled with self-loathing and doubt. I struggled with guilt: Did I eat something that triggered his early birth? Did I miss some kind of physical sign from my body? Was it all that bike riding? I was honest enough with my son's NICU nurses to bring my questions up, and was quickly assured it was just a turn of fate. From what I understand, my body had developed an infection, and my body's response was to get the baby out so he wouldn't be harmed. Pumping helped me focus on the present. I had a clear picture of what I could do to ensure that my tiny son thrived. I felt empowered. I wasn't able to keep him safe in my womb, but I was able to nourish my son every day. I could have spent his time in the NICU crying (and I sometimes did), or mourning the loss of the birth experience I wanted for us, but I didn't. Instead, I felt a renewed sense of my motherhood as fate was redefining it for me on a daily basis—there was no "right" way to be a mother, just my way. The in-between was a land of ideals.

THE UNAPOLOGETIC NO /
SORAYA CHEMALY

For me, having children was like being run over by a small, fast locomotive. I had, by virtue of giving birth to a singleton and then twins, three babies under the age of three. To say my husband and I were not prepared and had no idea what we were doing would be the understatement of the century. While I knew that becoming a mother would change my life, I did not know how much.

Now, let me say this: I love my children and love being a mother. But what I really wasn't ready for was the avalanche of manic mothering norms that pervaded my life as a result. From the moment I woke up to the moment I fell asleep (note that I did not say, go to bed) I was doing *something*, and someone, somewhere was an expert in why I was doing it *wrong*. Bottles or breast. Work or no work. Co-sleep or no sleep. Too much stimulation. Not enough stimulation. Mozart on. Mozart off. Clean floor. Dirty floor. Pets or no pets. Shots or no shots.

Too much holding. Not enough holding. Nanny. No nanny. Day care. No day care. Bonding. No Bonding. Diapers. No diapers.

Being became a prolonged exercise in inadequacy, undertaken in a haze of sleep deprivation, cortisol and adrenaline. And that was just the mothering bit. I was also working. Outside of the home, which means for money. Deadlines, conference calls in bathrooms, meetings, overdue reports. And married. Thank God my husband loved me unconditionally and had a sense of humor. I fast became the quintessential not-only-can-you-have-it-all-but-also-you-*must*-have-it-all mother. Otherwise, what kind of woman were you?

When my children started school, however, opportunities for hyper-mothering exploded. After years of entertaining, and caring for toddlers and organizing various play dates, childcare, and schedules, I foolishly thought that school meant I would have *more* time. Instead, it introduced a new and unforeseen pressure: volunteering. I genuinely didn't know what I was doing with children in school. I'd never had children in school, so when it came to anything related to this new experience, I, mom-in-headlights, just did it. I showed up for every event, I solicited auction items, I sorted books for book fairs, I made class play costumes, I baked, I "sewed," and I showed up and showed up and showed up.

Until the Incident of the Corn Husk Dolls.

The Incident of the Corn Husk Dolls is what sent me over the edge, and for that I will be eternally grateful. Are you familiar with corn husk dolls? I wasn't either. They're a toy that little children in Colonial America used to make and play with. One year, I agreed to staff an activity table at our school's "Colonial Day"—an event where children, dressed in full costume, pretend to spend the day in Colonial America. A) I did not realize that not only the children, but also the parents (read, 99 percent mothers) dressed in colonial garb on that day. For no particular reason, I draw a personal line at reenacting. B) I also did not know that I was expected to buy an obscene amount of corn, husk it, and lay the husks out to dry on my nonexistent lawn so that the children could make "real" dolls, you know, "authentic dolls." I countered that, in an effort to be authentic, we should *all* then drink the colonial equivalent of beer all day, but this didn't work. After several panic-stricken phone calls and emails about corn husks from Colonial Day Committee Members, I ordered, for the ridiculously low cost of $30, 3,000 corn husks and delivered them to the school with a note that no other woman should have to think about this for several years.

And I never volunteered again.

Of course, the problem was of my own making. I said yes to everything because saying no made me feel an amorphous maternal guilt. Socialization does, after all, have its purposes. Playdate? Yes! Meeting at noon? Yes! Homemade Playdough? Yes! Fundraiser? Yes! Can you finish this project by Wednesday? Yes! Toddler ice skating? Yes! Soccer? Yes! Business trip? Yes! Homemade meals? Yes! Book fair? Yes! As the children got older and school and activities set in, I found myself driving the equivalent of the distance between Washington, D.C. and Chicago twice a week. I woke up one day and my hands were numb. Then my arms. It took six weeks and a slew of medical tests for doctors to tell me what I already knew—no, I did not have brain cancer. I had children and was tired. I spent years grappling with the expectation that I would just do—mother, work, food, volunteer, more mothering, more work, more food, more volunteering. And that there was no compensation other than the idea that somewhere, somehow, there would be a tacit seal of "good mother" approval.

I felt like a skirted flip book stick figure that someone else had drawn and that they were maniacally flipping. But I had done this to myself. I had totally internalized, in my state of early motherhood somatization, everything society threw at me about how to be. However, I wasn't doing it *by myself*. Everywhere I looked, women I knew were frantic, tired, engaged in contrived activities, exhausted by vigilance and maternal frenzy. What I saw around me, especially in schools, were women—talented, energetic, and smart—creating often largely inefficient activities either to compensate for workplace systems that made it as hard as possible and financially irrational for them to work or to complement the absences that these systems required once they'd become mothers. Whether they were stay-at-home moms, working part-time or full time, the pressures were the same and were magnified by volunteer culture. The cherry on top was that everyone believed this was all about individual "choices."

Now, I know that many women enjoy volunteer work and that volunteering is a kindness without which much that is good in the world would not happen. This is not to denigrate the truly valuable work that volunteers do. The problem is not volunteering per se. It's the nature of our volunteer culture, particularly in the way it is enmeshed with mothering. Volunteering is a highly gendered activity. It is both fed by and perpetuates our country's sex-segregated workforce and persistent wage gap.

Women volunteer more than men. According to a Bureau of Labor Statistics report released in March 2012, there was even an uptick in volunteering marked by a gender gap. Women between the ages of thirty-five and forty-four, with at least one child, are the most likely to volunteer. These same women also tend to be college graduates.[1]

The most frequent anecdotal explanation I hear is, "The men have to work and be the breadwinners." What about single women?

Talk about an outdated idea whose time has long passed. While the nature of work and family has rapidly changed in the past forty years, volunteering has not. More than half of the labor force is women, and women are now the breadwinners in 40 percent of households. Men have not taken up the volunteering slack, and volunteering, for many women, is part of being a Good Mother.

Good Mothers fill schools and other organizations that benefit hugely from their unpaid labor. Many schools would come to a grinding

---

[1] "Volunteering in the United States 2012," *Bureau of Labor Statistics*, 23 Feb. 2013, http://www.bls.gov/news.release/volun.nr0.htm

halt if it were not for a largely female cadre of unpaid, talented workers. Mothers staff various offices, raise massive amounts of money, organize events, chair committees, run field trips, function as accountants, and substitute for teachers. They should be compensated for their work.

Every time they aren't, or volunteer cultures are dominated in gross disproportion by women, they perpetuate a system whereby women's work is invisible and unpaid.

At one point, a friend of mine—by virtue of having once been a senior expert in the finance securities sector, was asked to organize potluck dinner finances because she was "good with numbers." As an artist (I was a painter—of canvases, not walls), I was asked to paint stage sets and furniture because I was so "good with paint." Somehow, both she and I and millions of other women are expected to step up and provide hundreds of hours of work for free and that idea is compounded by the idea that that's what certain Good Mothers do.

School cultures are a microcosm of our economy. This donated "maternal labor" credit that gets applied to school budgets substantively contributes to an already unconscionable lifetime wage gap and sex segregation by devaluing all of our work. The same way that school budgets don't take this workforce into account, our Gross Domestic Product doesn't take the work women do as mothers (and a slim few men as fathers) and homemakers into account either. It is, technically, "leisure time." It's called "nonmarket household production" and it is just "too hard" to measure. Imagine that. Somehow we measure all kinds of other things just fine. If we valued women's work at home and as volunteers, we'd have to reconsider the biases inherent to our workforce and the decisions that go into women's and men's "choices" regarding work, childcare, and flexibility. We'd have to think about the fact that women are made financially vulnerable by these systems in ways that men are not.

The scenarios I'm describing are usually associated with problems of affluent, mainly white women who, for the most part, can afford to not work full time. However, as a *USA Today* analysis of the Bureau of Labor Statistics study explained, "Women of all ages, educational levels, and races volunteer more than men with the same demographic characteristics. Men volunteered at a rate 6.4 percentage points lower. And their participation was almost unchanged from the year before."[2]

Volunteer cultures illustrate problems that pervasively affect all women to varying and more extreme degrees. Most women are not in this category of staying at home and donating their time. Many feel the conflict, stress, and pressure of not being able to participate actively in volunteer cultures that become, in essence, daddy-subsidized hierarchies of women who can donate their time. I think the result is often a subtle race and class divide in school communities. On the other hand, I also understand the complexity of what it means to be an African American mother in this country who *can* volunteer, what that represents in historical terms and how different this experience can be for women of color. However, I believe that systems whereby women's labor is so massively discounted do us all a disservice and warrant greater discussion.

So, after three years trying to figure this out, I reread my worn Marilyn Waring bible, *If Women Counted,* and when next asked to sit on a school committee made up entirely of well-intentioned and hard-working women, I explained, with a smile, that I thought the spouses of these women should do it instead. Everyone laughed because it was such an absurd suggestion. Then I explained that their unpaid work bummed me out and went through my reasoning. I received uncomfortable blank stares, and a few wry smiles, but no one really asked me again.

Last Spring, my husband and I attended a school event where parents were asked to come see their children perform and eat lunch with

---

[2] Brian Tumulty, "Women are the Driving Force Between Higher Volunteerism Rate", *USA Today,* March 3, 2012, http://usatoday30.usatoday.com/news/health/story/2012-03-12/women-are-driving-force-between-higher-volunteerism-rate/53500042/1

them. I sat at a table with eight men and one other woman. Ten mothers staffed two buffet tables where kids lined up with plates, eager to eat. When lunch was served, one of the men at my table, in contravention of the request that children be allowed to eat first, got up to get his lunch. When he was asked to wait by a mother routing children toward the tables, he loudly, pointedly, and rudely proclaimed, "Some of us have *work* to get back to." The truth is, he only said out loud what many people still think. That's what complementary roles for men and women means, after all.

He eventually got to the buffet tables. A literal assembly line of mothers served him his lunch. My daughters, quietly absorbing as children do, life lessons from their environments and the behavior of the adults in them, understood exactly why I was not one of them.

I explained what I was doing and why to my children, who could not care less if I painted stage sets, or bought cupcakes instead of made them. Equally important, I learned to say no to anything I could not or would not or did not want to do, and I did so unapologetically. No excuses, no explanation. It's a too-late-in-life-acquired skill that I now happily apply to everything. A friend calls it, all caps, my UNAPOLOGETIC No. I am always civil, but when asked if I would spend six hours sorting books or decorating tables, I smile and say, "No, thanks," and leave it at that. Among the other things I've learned as a mother, is that women continue to explain way too much.

PARENTING WITHOUT A ROPE /
HEATHER HEWETT

tHE THIRD TIME MY DAUGHTER ALMOST DIED from a sip of milk was entirely my fault.

It was a late afternoon on a hot summer weekend in 2010. My six-year-old daughter ran around the backyard with her little brother while my husband and I cooked dinner. Mark grilled, and I chopped vegetables. Very 1950s. I carried plates and glasses to the deck while the kids laughed and screamed. We sipped white wine. I felt myself relaxing into the evening.

I poured drinks for the kids. Cow's milk for Liam and soy milk for Jessie—because of her dairy allergy.

I set their glasses down beside their placemats, making a careful mental note to remember who was sitting where. I realized I'd forgotten the margarine and went back inside, where Mark was cutting the grilled chicken.

I carried the margarine and a plate full of food back to the deck. As I opened the door, I heard a scream.

Jessie was pushing her chair back from the table, her eyes wide with terror. "My mouth is burning!" She coughed and spit. "It's spicy! It's spicy!"

My brain jerked out of its serene state. Jessie was sitting at Liam's place. Where I thought he would sit. Where he sat the night before. Jessie's skin was turning an alarming shade of red. I turned to Liam, who looked at me.

Jessie screamed again.

"You gave me Liam's milk! You gave me Liam's milk!"

She threw up.

"Oh my God," I said, unable to move.

"Get the EpiPen!" yelled Mark.

The events that followed will be familiar to most parents of children with anaphylactic allergies: the taut moment of plunging an enormous needle into a screaming child; of trying to breathe while reciting important numbers (911, our street address); of being pierced by the wail of an ambulance descending upon us; of listening to the sudden silence that wrapped itself around us.

As the ambulance pulled away with my husband and daughter, I looked down at my three-year-old son and tried to remember what to do. I needed to gather things. Items we might need: clothes, books. Food.

Our dinner lay untouched on the patio table.

I could see Liam working through what had just happened. "It wasn't Jessie's milk," he explained to me. "It was my milk. She drank the wrong milk."

"I know, sweetie," I said, holding back tears and cursing myself under my breath. "It was an accident."

But I didn't really believe myself. I knew exactly who to blame.

• • •

A friend of mine, a mother of two kids who are allergic to more foods than my daughter, believes that food allergies provide much-needed perspective on the whole parenting project. For example, sugar. She is a committed organic/locavore/foodie who just can't get worked up about sugar anymore. "So what?" she said to me one day, as her two sons munched on Skittles at the playground. "As long as it doesn't kill them."

It's true that certain things recede in importance, and it becomes much easier to resist the ideals of the Good Mother. *Okay, so my daughter's hair isn't brushed and she hasn't showered all week. But at least she has safe and healthy food to eat.* I've learned to accept being a "good enough" mom in many areas.

Embracing less-than-perfect mothering is one thing, but negligent mothering is entirely different.

To be sure, most of the time I am not a negligent parent, yet I have not always maintained the vigilance necessary to keep my daughter safe. The stakes are high when your daughter has life-threatening allergies to seven major foods, plus asthma and Celiac disease.

The first piece of evidence: the milk mix-up.

Shouldn't I have paid more careful attention? Why did I let down my guard? And why the hell was I drinking a glass of wine while cooking dinner?

The second piece of evidence: the time that Jessie drank from a sippy cup in the fridge that the nanny swore contained soy milk. We ended up in the hospital.

Why did I believe that nanny? Did we let our attachment to her outweigh my daughter's safety?

The third piece of evidence: my inability to give my daughter a shot of epinephrine in either of the above instances. Both times, her life was saved by paramedics and my husband.

Why was I so afraid of giving her an injection? What if someone else had not stepped in and saved her?

"It could have happened to anyone," Mark said to me after the milk mix-up. "Stop blaming yourself."

But I couldn't help it. I replayed the scene in my head, again and again.

Because when you have a child with life-threatening allergies, you can't let down your guard. Not for an instant.

And so I am haunted by my failures and my lapses. By the "what ifs." They terrify me.

Few women can escape the Good Mother. From the photos of celebrity moms to the articles in parenting magazines, she is everywhere. Our culture endlessly produces messages about what we must do in order to join her ranks, and what happens when we fail. The resulting range of acceptable behavior is about as wide as a slender, steep path up the side of a mountain.

For some of us, like me, the path narrows even further because of our situations. It's as if I'm pressing against a rocky wall on one side and leaning away from a plunging cliff on the other. Against my will, I'm climbing without a rope.

The directions I'm given about how to proceed seem to conflict. On the one hand, I need to exert vigilance and control; on the other, I need to let go. These mixed messages collide inside my brain, and I hesitate.

The result? Sometimes, my daughter isn't perfectly safe. I've put her in charge of her own EpiPen, and so it is forgotten at movie theaters, birthday parties, and parks—leaving her without the medication that has saved her life multiple times. Then there was the time that I got confused between her maintenance inhaler and her emergency inhaler, which meant that she wasn't taking the proper asthma medication for months. During this time, the poor kid ended up in the hospital twice, once on Christmas Day.

If only I could embrace my inner slacker mom—but I can't. Because this stuff *matters*. Unlike most moms, I don't have much of a margin for error. One misstep and we go plunging down.

Other times I know I'm doing my job, such as the afternoon I passed out hand wipes to twenty four-year-olds at a pizza party and made sure that each and every kid wiped her hands. Or the summer I dropped my daughter off at sleepaway camp and never left; her multiple allergies made the newly minted nurse feel "nervous." I remind myself that I've spent hours talking with teachers, principals, nurses, religious education counselors, camp directors, babysitters, and other parents about how to keep my daughter safe. But even in these moments, I can feel myself treading a different kind of line. The line that stands between good mothers and overprotective, neurotic ones.

You know, the "crazy" moms.

Deep down, I feel crazy too. But I don't want to be put into this category. I want to be reasonable. And so I temper myself, and at times keep quiet when maybe I shouldn't.

I have stayed silent while forty kids were shaking Ziploc bags filled with milk in order to make ice cream (a parent-led science project) in my daughter's classroom. I just didn't have the heart to ask these parents not to bring their project into school. They had called me ahead of time to suggest that I bring soy milk for Jessie's plastic bag, and they were very enthusiastic. Plus, it wasn't like I was spending any of my free time coming up with super-cool science projects for kids.

I have refrained from asking the other parents in my daughter's class not to bring in cupcakes for their children's birthdays. For holidays. For class parties. The list goes on.

I have worried that asking other parents *not to do this* would be seen as evidence that I was too pushy or overbearing or overly sensitive, that someone might feel I was being "unreasonable" to expect that other kids should alter their behavior—or lose a special learning opportunity—because of Jessie.

In none of these cases did I feel that my daughter's safety was truly imperiled. She wasn't eating the ice cream, after all. But I felt nervous. I worried about bags rupturing and milk spilling all over the place and Jessie feeling unsafe and generally left out. All of which came to pass, by the way. And in the end she was fine—of course she was fine—but maybe that's not all I was worrying about.

Maybe I didn't want her difference to mean her exclusion.

Maybe that's why I don't always speak out when I wish I could.

Maybe I want some of the other adults in the room to open their eyes and see what's going on.

In a world where food appears everywhere—every social gathering, classroom, and celebration—anxiety about social exclusion complicates the fear that my daughter might brush up against death. And so Mark and I have made choices, when we could, to let Jessie be a part of things and learn to live with her own anxiety, to recognize the difference between being uncomfortable and being unsafe.

I've had to learn to recognize this difference myself.

It helps to travel this road with another parent, to have someone with whom I can talk these things over. It helps to have a daughter who is growing up and taking control of her own life, bit by bit. The day that Jessie took one bite of fish and felt her throat closing, and told me clearly that she needed an EpiPen—and I gave her one—was a day of triumph.

I might have been trembling, but I placed my faith in my daughter's absolute certainty. Her beautiful moon face, brown eyes fixed upon me. *Now.*

Who was this amazing girl child in front of me? So preternaturally calm. So fearless.

She has made this journey easier, my daughter. She has made it possible for me to unclench my grip, little by little, to focus my energies on working with the school nurse and other adults to make sure they can recognize allergic reactions, use an EpiPen, and form an invisible if imperfect safety net around her. And I've felt my fears recede, little by little, as my daughter gains confidence in her ability to find her own path.

She's restless to rise above these cliffs, this one.

And then it occurs to me. Maybe she feels safe because I've been climbing, too.

Maybe it's just my perspective: I've been looking down instead of up. I haven't realized that my daughter is ready to soar.

All parents know the fear of losing their children. Whether or not we acknowledge it, we feel its shadow. We see it pass before us when we glimpse a child with cancer, or when our teenagers pass their driving test.

Seven years ago, a child drowned in our neighborhood pond in the middle of winter. He had taken a neighbor's dog for a walk, so proud of his new responsibility, but they strayed out onto thin ice. I didn't know the mother, but months later a friend told me that she had been seen at the local coffee shop. I was haunted by the thought of this woman, sitting alone at a table, sipping coffee and gazing out the window. It was her only child.

If we're lucky, we don't have to face this possibility. We push it away and bargain with God and cross our fingers.

Having a child with food allergies is no different. It's only that some of us are tempted—at least I am—by the thought that we can control every detail of our children's environment, in part because that is what is asked of us. Perfection becomes an expectation. We begin to secretly hope that maybe we can protect our children forever.

This, of course, is an impossible dream.

I want to reach out to that mother in the coffee shop. I want to say, it was not your fault. We are not in control of the winter, the dog pulling the child, the ice. I want to put my arms around her, to comfort her sorrow, to cry along with her.

It seems easy enough, this work of rejecting the myth of the Good Mother and embracing the good-enough mom. But to understand how difficult this task truly is—and, perhaps, how necessary—one must peer over the edge into the abyss while trying to remain calm.

We must hold our children close, and then we must let them go.

MAMA DON'T COOK /
CARLA NAUMBURG

I T'S NOT JUST THAT I CAN'T COOK. It's that I really don't *want* to. I've never been interested in any aspect of food preparation—from recipe planning to grocery shopping to the actual cooking. I find it all simultaneously tedious and overwhelming, a chore that is significantly less enjoyable for me than washing dishes or folding laundry. Given the choice, I would rather scrub dried grease off every last plate and pot left over after a ten-course meal than prepare said meal.

Genetically, it shouldn't be this way. My father is a decent cook; he prides himself on his Eggs Benedict recipe, and he even completed a course in French cooking when I was young. My mother raised me on a healthy diet of *Yan Can Cook* and Jacques Pepin reruns, but she didn't need their advice or recipes. Her cooking style is more intuitive, no instructions or timers required. She somehow knows just how much oregano to add, just how long to leave the roast in the oven, and her meals always come out perfectly. Yet it would seem that I have inherited neither the desire nor the ability to cook that my parents possessed. Given that I am a reasonably functional person in most other areas of my life—I keep a fairly neat house, I can knit, I've got two graduate degrees, and I've even driven myself across the country multiple times—it's hard to accurately describe this particular deficit to others who don't struggle in the same way I do.

I suppose it's not unlike how I feel about math. I did well in other academic subjects, but when it came to algebra and pre-calculus, it just never clicked. I would memorize rules and write out equations, and study and practice, but nothing helped. Not unlike cooking, there is an internal logic and an art to the science of math, but four long years of classes didn't get me any closer to understanding it. While my classmates seemed able to find the patterns and consistency in what we were learning, I just kept going back to the textbook, searching for some piece of information that would finally bring it all together. I never found it, and my solutions were always a few digits off or had a negative number that should have been positive. Worst of all, the minute I completed each homework assignment or exam, everything I had worked so hard to learn would evaporate from my brain. Every time I walked into the classroom, it was as if I had to learn a new language all over again.

I feel the same way in the kitchen. I know there are rules, basic truths about food preparation that everyone seems to have learned but me. How was I supposed to know there were giblets wrapped in plastic and shoved inside the chicken? And what the hell are giblets anyway?

Even when I do learn some fundamental law of the kitchen, it never seems to make its way into my long-term memory. I remember my mother telling me once that carrots, celery, and onion are a classic base for French soups, but I can't recall what else she said. That may be the only cooking "rule" I know, but I have no idea how to apply it. Unlike my husband, I don't understand the role that various ingredients play in recipes, so I'm never sure which ones are expendable, which ones are replaceable, and which ones are absolutely necessary.

Not unlike my difficulties with math, no matter how many times I read a recipe, no matter how much I try to pay attention and follow the instructions properly, I always manage to screw it up. I burn the onions, I don't whisk the batter enough, I forget to turn the boiling soup down to a simmer. As a result, I've never successfully roasted a chicken. That's right. I'm a Jewish mother who has never fried a latke or made matzah ball soup. My aversion to cooking wasn't a problem before we had kids; my husband is a talented chef who reads cookbooks for fun and can prepare a delicious four-course meal without thinking twice. Whenever we hosted friends, he would cook while I would schmooze, and then after the meal, I would clean while he would relax with our guests. When he wasn't home to make dinner, I'd make a simple salad or fry an egg; I would snack on fruit, frozen burritos, and peanut butter and jelly sandwiches. It was good enough for me.

But now I am a mother of two young daughters, and apparently it's not good enough for them. Four years of being inundated by information from parenting books, online blogs, Twitter, Facebook, and comments from well-intentioned family and friends, has drilled into me precisely how, and what, Good Mothers feed their children. Everyone has a slightly different take on the matter, but the consistent message is that every meal needs to be fresh, healthy, homemade, and of course, delicious. That's a lot to take in, especially for someone who still doesn't entirely understand the difference between baking and broiling.

To be honest, I can't totally blame it on the media or other mothers. I wasn't prepared for the vulnerability of parenting, for the intense fear that I might somehow fail at the most important, most meaningful adventure of my life. I was overwhelmed by the sheer volume of advice; I had no way of discerning what mattered and what didn't, whether or not I really needed to worry about BPA in water bottles or mold in humidifiers or the supposed dangers of supplementing with formula. My intense desire and self-induced pressure to become the Good

Mother resulted in a myopic focus on my greatest parenting-related flaw: my inability to cook. At the same time that I stopped worrying about whether or not my toddler was gobbling dirt or licking the walls, I became obsessed with the rest of her diet. I started paying attention to what the voices of the Good Mothers in my communities (both virtual and real) were telling me about the *right* way, the only way, to feed a child.

Fresh, locally-grown organic fruits and vegetables represent the bare minimum of acceptability, regardless of whether or not they are even available and affordable.

Apparently, I also need to cook a wide range of colorful meals, which include the aforementioned fruits and veggies, as well as whole grains, wild-caught fish, and lean, grass-fed, cage-free, organic chicken and meat. Yet it doesn't stop there; I'm supposed to happily prepare these meals in creative and visually pleasing ways, with my four-year-old and two-year-old by my side in the kitchen, eagerly learning how to cook from me. Once we've created a perfect meal of turkey/hummus/tomato/avocado whole-grain roll-ups adorned with Hello Kitty toothpicks and cucumber stars and a side of low-fat yogurt topped with homemade granola and fresh blueberries, I am to sit at the table with my children, enjoying our meals while we discuss the events of the day and debate topics of interest to us all.

My daughters' selective food preferences (to put it nicely) and their desire to subsist entirely on noodles and bunny crackers aside, the reality is that I am not that mother. I am never going to be that mother. I'd rather scrub a toilet than go to a farmer's market. The greens that come in our farm-share each week (courtesy of my husband) look like weeds to me and lie untouched until he does something with them. The thought of preparing yet another dinner every night leaves me in a state of mild panic and occasional rage several times a week. I count the days until the weekend, when I can happily relegate all food-related tasks to my husband, who creates tasty, healthy meals for the entire family in the amount of time I often spend staring blankly at the contents of the refrigerator, frozen in my anxiety about what to feed my girls.

But I want to be a Good Mother; try as I might, I can't let go of the idea that I simply won't be one unless I somehow transform myself into that mother in the online cooking videos I have watched over and over again—you know her, she's the one who smiles into the camera as she sautés vegetables from her own garden while her toddler sits happily in the high chair next to her, eagerly shoving lentils and spinach into his mouth. I've somehow convinced myself that unless I find my inner Julia Child, my daughters' taste buds will never properly develop, rendering them completely unable to ever appreciate subtle tastes and complex flavors. Even if they do somehow manage to survive their deprived childhoods, my girls will probably grow up to be obese and sick, unable to become productive, capable members of society. They'll never hold down jobs or develop and maintain healthy romantic relationships. They will, quite simply, never be happy. All because I don't cook.

Every other month or so, I recommit myself to the process, not unlike starting yet another diet on the first of the year. I manically create online calendars and color-coordinated notecards for the purposes of meal-planning; I sign up for websites that will send me a list of recipes (along with a handy shopping list) each week, and I buy cookbooks and recipe apps for my iPhone. I convince myself that if I just work hard enough, I'll finally get it right this time. I become determined that this is the week, the month, the year, that I will learn to cook, that I will enjoy cooking, that I will finally become a Good Mother. I fantasize about bringing a homemade vegetarian lasagna or artichoke dip to a potluck, instead of yet another fruit salad. I linger over the brightly colored plastic Bento Boxes at the end of the grocery aisles, smiling smugly to myself as I fantasize about all of the amazing leftovers I'll be sending for the girls' school lunches. I imagine my daughters happily eating frittatas and casseroles each night for dinner, even though a) they would never, ever eat something like that, and b) I'm not entirely sure what those are.

I spend the next week calling my husband from the grocery store because I don't know what leeks are, much less how to count them or which end you eat. After a few days of faking my way through a conversation with the guy behind the meat counter (how the hell am I supposed to know how much ground beef I want?) and stumbling my way through the kitchen, chopping and stressing, bitterly sautéing when I'd rather be building Lego towers with the girls, I give up. There are just so many times in a week when I can swallow my pride and wait for my husband to come home and save the half-raw chicken or rescue the roasted asparagus that I somehow managed to screw up (yet again). He's very kind about it, and he even genuinely appreciates my hard work when we finally sit down to the meal. Nonetheless, I can't help but feel deeply inadequate when that happens—I don't rely on my husband in such a helpless way in any other aspect of our relationship, and I just can't tolerate it.

So, once again, I ditch the websites and cookbooks, and the girls are back on a diet of noodles, steamed broccoli and cauliflower, cheese sticks, and blueberries. They'll eat veggie burgers and dip baby carrots in hummus, and snack on peanuts, raisins, watermelon and yogurt. It may be healthy enough, but does that make me a Good Mother, or just good enough? As the smiling lady on the online video reminds me, a good diet isn't just about feeding their bodies, it's about nourishing their little souls. And that means not only do I need to feed my daughters fresh sugarsnap peas, but I also have to teach them how to cook them, and where they came from (and clearly "the freezer aisle" is not an acceptable answer).

It's just not going to happen. It pains me to admit it, but I'm not interested in watching a tomato plant grow or learning the difference between rosemary and thyme. I'm slowly coming to terms with the reality that I won't be the one to teach my daughters to cook, that their childhood memories won't be associated with the smells of Mama's homemade brisket or freshly-baked cookies. I'm getting more comfortable with sending my older daughter to school with the same lunch every day (decidedly not in a Bento Box), not only because she actually likes—and eats—her sunbutter and jelly sandwich, her cheese and grapes, but also because I dread the thought of having to come up with new ideas every day.

Perhaps there's another lesson buried in all of this, for both me and my daughters. I used to think of myself as a mother who lacked a vital parenting skill, one who just gave up when things got hard. As my girls grow up, I have witnessed the unfolding of their innate strengths and strong personalities and preferences. It's given me a different perspective on the value of acknowledging my own abilities and deficits, and working with them rather than constantly fighting to be someone I'm not. Quite simply, I'm not a cook. I never will be. The truth is that I'm happier not only when I stay out of the kitchen, but also when I let go of the self-doubt and shame about all of it. While I plan to encourage my daughters to try new challenges and step outside their comfort zones, I might also gently suggest that they back away from a particularly solid brick wall, rather than repeatedly beating their heads against it. I've learned the hard way that you rarely break through, and more often than not, you just end up with a headache.

So, I'm working hard to turn off the voices in my head that criticize the scrambled eggs and veggie nuggets I feed the girls for dinner. I've stopped visiting the cooking websites and Pinterest boards, and I ignore the Facebook pictures of lamb ribs with roasted fennel and home-grown heirloom tomatoes. I'm grateful for weekends and nights when my husband is home in time to cook, and for the holiday meals we share at my in laws' house. Perhaps more importantly, I've started paying attention to the subtle comments my friends make about getting take-out or sticking a frozen pizza in the oven. Yes, most of them can cook better than I can, but that doesn't mean they always do. Apparently, I'm not the only mother who doesn't want to spend her life in the kitchen.

I know that my daughters have a healthy diet, even if I don't always (or ever) cook meals worthy of tweets or status updates. I remind myself that I'm a Good Mother in so many other ways. I read books with the girls, and I tuck in their baby dolls with my kitchen dishrags (let's be honest here, it's not like I really need them for anything else). I spell out words, one letter at a time so my preschooler can write them out, and I comfort my toddler, who is endlessly frustrated that she can't do everything her sister can. I set limits, enforce rules, and keep the girls safe and clean. We go for walks and play in the dirt outside, and I bring Passover and Hanukah stories and crafts to share with their preschool and daycare classes. We talk about their feelings, their wishes, and their worries. Then we share a quesadilla and apple slices for dinner. It may not be a roasted chicken with asparagus and couscous, but that doesn't mean it's not Good Mothering.

THE HALLOWED LIFE
OF AN AGNOSTIC MOTHER /
VICTORIA BROOKE RODRIGUES

J ONAH IS CUDDLED IN DINOSAUR-PRINT pajamas, smelling like half-days of preschool, and calling me to prayer again. Only a few months ago, this was the hardest part of my day: my son requesting not a bedtime story, not sleep-eluding snacks, drinks, or kisses. Only an unassuming sigh as he would curl his knees into his chest: "Prayer, Mama?"

I "grew up Catholic," as I often hear other non-committals say of themselves. This means that I attended Mass throughout childhood, received every sacrament because it was expected of me, and most importantly, panicked in the back row of catechism classes waiting for someone to call me out: big, giant faker.

I was "agnostic" long before I learned the term's meaning; I simply hid from others the hopes and doubts I had concerning any form of God or afterlife. I felt uneasy with the contrast between Christ's teachings and the actions and beliefs of Western "Christian" culture many years before I would recognize it as a common touchstone in religious, political, and social commentaries. I couldn't understand why God wouldn't show me He was really there. I couldn't understand how *thou shall not kill* could be subjective. I still can't. Every night when I snuggled with Jonah and groped for a prayer, I wondered if it would be the night he might call me out: big, giant faker.

However, there was never a doubt that my son would spend his Sundays in Mass. My husband is no undecided; his Bible and Rosary are conditioned with the oil of his fingertips. I go to Mass every Sunday, not out of deference to him or my own ambivalence, but because I see in my husband's faith something I have always envied, something I want our son to have a chance at if he so chooses. While there will always be room for questions and doubts in our home, I want Jonah to have the opportunity to explore his spirituality through the faith of our families' cultures. I also want Jonah to have a visceral connection to the mysticism and iconography passed through his heritage, traced back to Hispanic, Spanish, and Portuguese roots, now growing among the *penitentes* and *retablos* of the American Southwest.

For myself, I desired to continue the tradition of my women-ancestors, for whom enacting daily works of faith was often their most liberated and mindful contribution to their family. While my grandmothers and great-aunts were required to ask their husbands' permission to allow a visit from a friend, while they lobbied for money to take to the grocery store, and while they were asked to enforce rules for the children at the father's insistence, there was one area of their lives where they were head of household: implementing works and rituals of faith. My grandmothers lit candles on the correct days, touched us with Holy water, and heckled Godparents. My grandmothers would not serve dinner until the prayer was spoken, and grandfathers showed uncommon remorse if they crossed such lines. While I was pained at the inequity they suffered, I wanted the womanly part of moral compass and spiritual guide. I wanted my son to come to me for answers before I believed I had any to give.

Yet I feared our return to church. Not Catholicism particularly; I have sorted through my anger with the Church. Time spent in various government and academic bureaucracies has lightened the burden of dogma and ritual, a satire on the human pursuit of order and meaning. I've seen sufficient violence and persecution from the hands of everyday people against other everyday people to know radicalism can spring from believing in anything at all: religion, politics, philosophies, traditions, soccer teams. Catholicism is the easily parodied Big Bad Wolf of belief systems, but in reality no more dangerous than other countless belief-centered elements of society through which we will help Jonah navigate.

What I did fear was allowing church or anything outside our home to become the centerpiece of Jonah's morals, values, and understanding of the world. Sure, we regularly focused on ideas like the golden rule at home, but I worried that the power of Mass—the congregation booming in unison, the repetition of Christian-centric ideas—would overrule any impact I could have on Jonah's perspective as his *mother*. I worried Mass might create an alienating schism between Jonah's understanding of the world and mine, the canyon between the faithful and the doubtful. I was afraid that he would see Christianity as the only way up the proverbial mountain and later realize his mother was taking the scenic route. I feared his theoretical future judgment. I even feared his theoretical future pity.

Praying with Jonah began when he asked, after a long Mass, "What is Church?" "Church is where we pray," I said. That night, when I tucked him in, Jonah asked, "What is Pray?" "Pray is when you ask for help when you need help, and think of all the things you are thankful for," I told him.

Prayer began as a self-contained event I controlled. Jonah and I snuggled close and recollected various blessings, saying thank you to no one in particular. We focused on gratitude rather than the gratifier, because I knew no other way to simultaneously maintain honesty and satisfy Jonah's need to connect with life's abstractions: the most important, most difficult things to explain to a child.

But the simplicity of prayer ended when we moved from our church's cry room, with its muffled speakers and crying babies, to the main congregation where Jonah could clearly hear the repetition of Mass every Sunday. He was particularly fascinated by the chanting, rhythmic, "Our Father," recited in harmony. At night, Jonah asked to say the "Our Father."

What is "hallowed be thy name"? What are trespasses? What is temptation? Suddenly I was Jonah's values-and-abstractions dictionary, and I worried he would find my pages scrawled in illegible, circular rhetoric.

Who am I to explain holy?

The first few nights of this routine were anguish. I would lie next to Jonah formulating my answer, time in which he would repeat the question, as preschoolers will do. "What is hallowed? What is hallowed? Mommy, *what is hallowed?*" Of course, after I tinkered out my best stab at hallowed, the definition needed to be defined. What is honor, respect, revere?

Slowly, the routine eased. I was able to connect abstractions to real events and feelings in Jonah's world, and build from there.

After weeks of hand-made prayers and hard-fought explanations, I realized that *my* prayer had been answered. Jonah would not sit silently and absorb a world view by repetitive osmosis. Instead, Mass forced Jonah and I to sit and hash out these ideas together. The outside introduction of "Truths" and *truths* showed me that, if I were to fail at my duty to identify and initiate discussions of important ideas, the repetition of laden words on Sunday mornings guaranteed we would sort them out on Sunday nights.

However, even in this I created an uneasy peace between the potential faith of my son and the woman breathing its words at bedtime. I was taking comfort in our prayer sessions as if the insights of a preschooler could cement his heart for a lifetime. Someday, if he follows down the Christian road, he will know the idealized mothers of the Bible, the women on whom Western, Christian models of feminine perfection are built. These are the women who greet God's requests with *thy will be done*. These are the women who give completely their minds, bodies, and souls. My existential work with Jonah could not be more unlike their ecstatic suspension; my every word is tainted with self-interest. I profess the intention of raising him with an open heart and mind, but truthfully I am asking him to understand belief as I do, *my will be done*. I am no divine mother; I am instead my son's namesake.

When the prophet Jonah refused to deliver God's message to the Ninevites, God gave Jonah time to reconsider his faith while trapped in the belly of a great sea creature. I, too, am refusing to pass on all of the messages. Instead of a fish dripping stomach, I am trapped under a head of never-cut hair with a sleep-twitching arm across my belly. All the same, I, too, cannot leave this place without reconciling my relationship to a creator and my created.

I struggled. Some nights I cut explanations short, unable to resolve competing feelings. Some nights I strictly gave my own interpretations, self-interested but true. Some nights I let catechism in, self-interested but true. And in this way, I learned about being a new kind of Head of Spiritual Household, one who is defender not of The Faith but of the faiths.

I learned that I was not the kind of mother who would let my children be told what to believe, by a church or by myself. I learned to have confidence in my uncertainty. I began to feel comfort not from strengthened faith, but from a promise of this fraught traverse of my son's soul and my own. The struggle is an attempt to merge faith and doubt into a single spiritual life. The comfort is in the potential that Jonah will have his own struggle outside of both the Church and the Mother.

I was able to become the matriarchal spiritual guide in the same moment I ceased to desire it. Doubt can be as much of a foundation as faith.

In the story of the prophet, God forgives Jonah for refusing his instructions, only for Jonah to commit yet another transgression. Jonah sits outside of the city to which he originally refused to go, Nineveh. There he has finally preached his doomsday prophecy. With Nineveh in site, he prays to God to destroy the city, lest his status as foreseer and prophet come into question, not to mention his God's reputation as the ultimate power of judgment. Jonah is unquestioning in his self-righteousness. The verses race with the excitement in his heart. The people within the city, on the other hand, decide to ask for forgiveness in case God *might* be merciful. Their words translate roughly to what so many of the faithful and the doubtful say every day of God: *Who can tell? Who knows?* Ultimately, God spares the uncertain Ninevites and scolds the devout and absolute follower, who cared more for his certitude than his fellow man. Perhaps what my son needs more than a faithful mother is one who is starting in the same place he is now, in the place of *who can tell?*

Now, Jonah and I often redefine the same ideas, night after night. Sometimes I'm not sure either of us totally understands, but there are signs we are getting there. One afternoon, Jonah came into my office and saw the dog collar I keep on my wall as a memento of a beloved pet from my childhood. After I explained the significance of this talisman, Jonah said, "That's hallowed." Surely a fraying collar is not in the traditional definition of hallowed, but it fits in the spiritual framework Jonah and I are building together. We both know that, like a cross, you don't spend twenty years with a collar tacked to your wall unless you believe in it.

In true agnostic style, you won't find me asserting that these worshiping Sundays and prayerful nights will ensure my son will appreciate the depth of his father's faith or the pain of his mother's doubt. Even where I construct a semblance of belief, I leave room for doubt. But mothering, like faith, is in large part living with a lack of control over what we crushingly desire to have in our command. The closest I have ever come to true religion is this resignation to toil toward an end, one which I have no real promise of and no undeniable proof, while begging from the world a kindness I have not seen it give anyone, all in concession to its infinite powers beyond me.

WHEN OUR HEARTS WALK OUTSIDE OF OUR BODIES /
JESSICA VALENTI

I'M THE KIND OF PERSON WHO USED TO scoff at overprotective moms—my own included. Whenever I didn't answer a phone call from my mother, the voicemails she left would get more frantic every hour that went by. (Keep in mind, this is when I was in my 20s—not some wayward teen.) The anxiety, the obsession, the never-ending worry . . . it all just seemed so pointless. Not to mention annoying. I made the decision never to do the same to my daughter. After all, chances are your kid is going to be fine.

Until they're not.

When I got pregnant with my daughter, Layla, I bristled at parenting ideologies that seemed to want to breed the kind of overprotectiveness I grew up with. Wear your baby or she won't feel attached to you! Breastfeed or her immune system will be weak! Are you scheduling your baby's tummy time for optimum stimulation? It was all just too much. I wanted to give my daughter the independence I felt I had so little of when I was growing up, and I knew these pressurized expectations were not ideal conditions to reach that goal. Not only did this overwhelming amount of advice seem to be stifling for kids, but for me as well. My mom always seemed so worn out by worry, I never wanted the same thing for myself. Instead, I planned to be Laid-Back Mom.

Then I had Layla, and the way she came into the world ensured that all of my best–laid-back plans on parenting were thrown out the window. In my twenty-eighth week of pregnancy, I developed pre-eclampsia. And a routine appointment with my ob-gyn quickly became a rush to the hospital, where I was promptly hooked up to IVs and told that I would be resting out the remainder of my pregnancy there. Unfortunately, the remainder of my pregnancy didn't end up being very long: within two days my liver started to fail and my daughter was born via an emergency c-section, mired in fear, pain, and confusion.

She was 2 pounds, 2 ounces; I wasn't able to see her for twenty-four hours, and it would be a week before I could hold her (and even then, just for a minute). Layla would be in the hospital for a little over two months, with ups and downs I never could have imagined. Suddenly, being over-involved and overprotective didn't seem so silly. It felt necessary.

I sat vigil at her incubator, even though she didn't spend much time awake and I couldn't do anything but talk to her and hold her hand. I watched the monitor obsessively, analyzing every beep and blip, worrying about every dip of her blood pressure or oxygen levels.

Sometimes, I felt useful being there. After all, it wasn't a nurse who noticed that Layla's eye was seeping and infected—it was me. And later, it would be me who reminded her nurses which eye needed caring for. All of a sudden, having an overprotective mother of my own came in incredibly useful. My mother noticed one day while visiting Layla that her isolette, or incubator, seemed cold. (The incubator was kept warm because Layla was too premature to be able to regulate her own body temperature.) The nurse hadn't realized that the heating mechanism had broken.

Advocating for your child takes on a whole new meaning when her health is at risk. We needed to ask questions about everything— every blood test, every x-ray, every invasive procedure. And I'm glad we did. The worrying I could have lived without; all it did was terrify me. But the truth is that my worrying was all that I had. It's what made me feel like I was in control of an uncontrollable situation.

Of course, most of this "overprotectiveness" wasn't really overprotectiveness at all—it was reasonable care and concern during a traumatic time. But the appropriate level of parenting worries and desire to protect Layla became more nebulous once she was able to come home. What was real worry and what was just my anxiety?

My husband and I started to fight about what constituted reasonable worry with a premature infant. What I saw as too-fast-breathing, he saw as her having a dream. He was okay if she didn't finish a meal, but I was obsessed with keeping her calorie count up.

In a way, we were both right. I still thought of her as needing special care, and he was concerned about setting a precedent that treated her as "sick" rather than "normal." We were both protecting her—just from different things.

Today, Layla is two years old and healthy. You would never know that she was premature or that she had health problems in the beginning of her life. We are getting back to normal.

What we went through is not the norm, I know that. Most parents won't have sick children, or a premature birth. Most won't have the same worries we did. But in a way, what we experienced in Layla's early life was just a heightened example of what all parents go through: being forced to accept a lack of control.

When we have kids, there's only so much we can do to protect them. We can't control if they get sick, if they get bullied, if the world doesn't work out the way we'd like it to for them. Most parents are able to push aside that frightening reality. Who wants to think about it, after all! But sometimes, in small ways, we're reminded and it's terrifying. The mere act of having a child means accepting that something you love deeply is out in the world and out of your control.

In the aftermath of tragedies like the Sandy Hook Elementary School massacre in Newtown, Connecticut, we're reminded all the more that, as President Obama so aptly noted in his memorial speech, "Having children means having our hearts walk around outside of our bodies."

So when I find myself scowling at some other mother's parenting style, or even being hard on myself, I remember that being "overprotective" is subjective—that at the end of the day, it's just a mostly reasonable response to the oh-so-scary act of having something exist in the world that you love more than yourself.

YES, I AM THAT SELFISH /
AVITAL NORMAN NATHMAN

MY SON TURNED FIVE THE YEAR that he really understood what it meant to "make a wish." Before then, when he stood over the flickering candles that topped his birthday cake, he would do it simply to indulge the relatives and friends who shouted for him to "make a wish!" He would pause briefly, gracing us with a huge smile and sparkling eyes as he blew his candles out, a bit of spit accompanying his breath. To him, it was just part of the ritual before getting to the good part—the sweet frosted reward of being born—rather than a chance to make a cherished wish.

Somewhere between the ages of four and five, all of that changed. During my own birthday party that year, when somebody reminded me to make sure my wish was a good one, my son looked at me curiously, as if he was sizing me up. After I'd blown out the candles and we had scarfed down the cake, he sat on my lap, nuzzling in closely.

"Ima," he whispered, his cake-scented breath tickling my ear. "What did you wish for?"

I perked up in surprise, wondering how he had finally made the connection between birthday candles and wishes, but decided not to push it. Instead, I answered him, somewhat.

"They say that if you share your wish, it won't come true."

He looked up at me with wide eyes and a slightly quivering lip. I gave him an extra squeeze before leaning down to whisper in his ear.

"I'll tell you, though. I wished for more cake!" My laughter sparked his, and we both broke down into a fit of giggles, effectively ending the conversation.

It wasn't the last of the wish-talk. As the year progressed, and we attended other birthday parties, I noticed that he paid close attention when the birthday boy or girl was instructed to make a wish. Then, without fail, once we were back in the car or on our bikes to head home, he would confide in me.

"I know what I want to wish for when I turn five. But I'm not telling!"

He declared this time and time again until finally we were only days from his birthday. I reconfirmed, for what felt like the hundredth time, exactly what type of cake he wanted: chocolate with vanilla frosting. We went over the guest list and what I had finally acquiesced to for his goody bags. And every so often during our birthday party discussions, he would remind me, with a look of glee on his face, that he had come up with the best birthday wish ever.

Eventually his birthday came and went in a blur of kids, presents, and of course, the cake. I watched as he scrunched up his newly five-year-old face before blowing out the candles, and wondered what he ended up wishing for. I didn't have to wait too long to find out. Later that night we were snuggling in bed when he burrowed in next to me, his voice dropping down to just above a whisper.

"Want to know what I wished for, Ima?" he asked. I nodded,

genuinely curious what this wish of all wishes could be. Was he hoping for a certain toy, a trip to someplace expensive, or perhaps the permission to eat candy for breakfast?

He looked me straight in the eye and without missing a beat, said, "I wished for you to have a baby."

My heart dropped into my stomach, and I felt like the worst mother ever as I choked out in a whisper that didn't quite reach his ears, "I'm sorry you wasted your wish."

I was never one of those women who dreamed up a house full of children running around while I coddled and cooed over them. In fact, I was never really one for young children at all. Despite all of that, I still knew that I wanted a family that extended beyond my husband and me. So we actually took the steps in planning to get pregnant, which ended up taking a little longer than we anticipated. But I dutifully took my temperature every day, and charted my cycles, and finally our little boy was conceived. It was worth it, and we were happy.

It was then, once my son was born, that I was able to start picturing the future, and it only ever involved the three of us: me, my husband, and our son. The thought of having a second child entered our minds, but only in a fleeting "do we have to?" sort of way.

Then it started. If I had thought that all the presumptive questioning (along the lines of "when are you getting married?" and "when are you having a baby?") would stop once I was legally hitched and had popped out one kid, I was wrong. Once our son turned two, the questioning began again. Only this time, they were less questions than they were opinions cloaked in concern.

"You're going to have another one . . . right?"

"He'd make an excellent older brother."

"But who will he play with?"

And, my absolute favorite:

"Who will help him take care of you when you're older?"

Time after time, I heard that having a second child would *really* complete our family, as if we were somehow unfinished with just the three of us. When our son was still young, we got the, "you might not want another one now, but when he gets older, you'll be wanting a baby!"

Our son did get older, and we still didn't want another baby. If anything, watching him grow up only solidified our desire to have just one. Not because it was hard, but because we actually felt full and complete as a family of three. Friends, relatives, and the occasional stranger still didn't believe us, thinking they knew better than us about how we wanted to form our family. Some even considered us "selfish" for not providing a sibling for our son to grow up with. Once, somebody even had the audacity to ask me, "Just one? What's the point?"

Our decision was not made lightly. My husband and I thought long and hard about whether *we* wanted to expand our family. But despite all the pressure we felt to expand, we decided we were perfectly happy and complete with our family of three.

There were a few folks that still didn't believe that we were serious. It got to the point where I almost photo-documented my IUD insertion just to show that, "Yes! We are that serious!"

Apparently we are also that "selfish." I continued to hear that sentiment with each passing year away from my son's birth, from people both close to me and those who were not.

I'd be lying if I said that those words didn't hurt just a bit. For a while I mistook the hurt for having made the wrong decision. I would studiously watch families of four or more whenever we went out, trying to make sure I hadn't glossed over something we were truly missing. I tried to better understand the feelings that bubbled to the surface as I watched young siblings play, and laugh, and share secrets together.

Countless nights I would find myself awake, lying restless in bed, trying to decide if I should march down to my midwife's office the next morning, demanding she remove the IUD, so my husband and I could begin working on kid number two later that night.

I would watch as my son delicately stroked the downy soft hair of a friend's new baby, unable to take his eyes from the gurgling little person in front of him.

Were we actually being selfish?

Mother's guilt crept in. The knowledge of my son's birthday wish seemed to compound it, gnawing away at my heart and sitting heavy in my belly.

He clearly wants a sibling so much. How could you be such a heartless mother? Kids are a joy! You should have just one more. Everyone would be happier.

Only, I knew that wasn't our truth. I knew that we were already happy. And that *he* was also a truly happy kid, despite his wish. His life, and ours, wasn't "less" because of not having more.

The five-year-old birthday wish has come up every so often since my son's party. Each time we talk about it, I explain how there are many different ways to make a family and that in addition to our actual family, we're lucky to have lots of friends that make up our extended one. His wish to be a big brother tends to now be on par with his wish to always eat ice cream for dinner—seemingly an amazing idea in the moment, but also easily forgotten.

Regardless of what other people may feel about my choices, I'm not really all that selfish, just different. And that's totally all right with me, and my happy family of three.

PART II

IN THE MAMA TRENCHES

THE GOOD ENOUGH MOTHER /
NERISSA NIELDS

mOTHERHOOD BRINGS OUT THE BEST and the worst in me. At my best, I am all presence, letting my eyes and ears and nose and heart be filled with the dazzling beauty and abundant energy and brilliant lightning storms that are my two children. I watch them run ahead of me, and I feast on their gaits. I hold them in my arms and breathe in the scent of their heads each morning as we sit on the kitchen couch and watch the sunrise and the birds come to the feeder. I listen intently as they tell me about their day, reveling in their creative grammar and diction. I write down what they say, "Bemember?" "Sank you, Mama," "I'm a wok, I'm a wok, I'm a wok star!"

And at my worst, I am worse than a control freak; I am a control monster, I am a control demagogue. I actually called my daughter a baby once when she fell on the floor for the fifth time in a row and kicked her legs in the air during violin practice.

Name-calling is a thing I swore pre-kid (PK) that I would never do. Losing my temper or exploding when the child broke something I loved or wrote with Sharpie on my grandmother's marble table top were also things I swore I'd never do. But parenthood brings me face-to-face with the parts of myself that are kind of duct-taped together, like the back of a drawer in the corner of the kitchen. PK, these parts weren't used much, but kids find these places, these drawers, and open and shut them, open and shut them until the duct tape comes unstuck. And I notice that the more these drawers get open and shut, the quicker I am to jump right to the default mode of anger.

I have wrestled my son into his clothes in the morning, him fighting me with every ounce of his thirty-two pounds, me wrapping my legs around him to get the t-shirt over his squirmy head. I am not proud of this. I hate myself, in fact, as I am doing it, yet I feel compelled. Why? Because I made a plan—to get him to school so I can get to work on time, to be specific. And in general, I think it's probably a good thing to make it clear that sometimes he's going to have to live with his disappointment. The parent stands for the whole world, and part of our job is to reflect back to the child how the world will react to his willfulness or adorableness.

In these moments, I have to remind myself that there is no such thing as a good mother. There is only the *good enough* mother.

Now, even as I write these words, I have a choir protesting in my head, or maybe over my left shoulder. "Of course there's such a thing as an empirically Good Mother. What about Carol? What about Sheila and Tracy? *What about Amanda Soule?*"

Surely there's a reason we even have the myth, right? It's those blasted women who seem to finesse every aspect of mothering—from breastfeeding until kindergarten and making their own juice-sweetened treats with kale snuck cleverly into everything, to spending the first five years of their children's lives on the rug with them, playing with cars and trains and teaching them to read. Or—this is what gets me feeling competitive and inadequate—parents who read (all the way to the end) the *Parent's Tao Te-Ching*, or Jon Kabat and Myla Zinn's *Everyday Blessings*; these are the same moms who sit on the edge of their child's bed in a state of pure gratitude, and wait, night after night, until those eyelids close—never feeling a pinch of resentment at how the ticking clock is cutting into their much-needed adult time; and most of all, these are the mothers who respond to temper tantrums and whining with endless patience, firmness, presence, and love.

With nary a piece of duct tape to speak of.

The reason this is so painful is because this is the way I *almost* parent, which I know is more than good enough. I buy *The Parent's Tao*, and I read along and nod my head vigorously when the writer says, "You can control your children/through threats and punishments/ and they will learn to fear." And then I tell my kids that if they don't hang up their jackets they won't get the cookies we just bought at the grocer's. I read the Kabat-Zinn's wonderful book about parenting as mindfulness practice, and I approach our family vacation as if it were an extended meditation retreat. "How present can I be?" I intone to myself on the airplane, and congratulate myself for focusing on my daughter's handwriting as she composes a letter to her best friend on the tray table next to mine. I sit on the beach helping my son build a sand castle and patiently mold the wet sand into turrets. I resist my iPhone for hours. And then at the end of the day I lock myself in the bathroom and gorge on Facebook, ignoring the calls of, "Mama? Are you still in there?" And I cringe in shame, thinking, *The Kabat-Zinns would never lock themselves in a bathroom—let alone be on Facebook. Let alone have an iPhone.*

But then I think of my friends (and Amanda Soule, the Kabat-Zinns, and the Taoists among us), and I am reminded of the great slogan, "Never judge another's outsides against your own insides." I have heard many stories from mothers I'd assumed to be beatific in which they thoroughly out themselves as just as impatient and haranguing as I am. This shocks and delights me every time, because it's hard to imagine that any of my friends, even those who complain about their kids' behaviors, ever feel as angry as I do.

If I were to be honest, what threatens me most is seeing a mother who actually *does* personify my own ideal: a fellow artist/writer/entrepreneur who seems to be raising her kids with the full force of her creative gifts. For example, a writer mom who is cowriting a book with her child. A musician mom whose daughter—let's just say "enthusiastically"—plays the violin part along with "I Am the Walrus" when asked to do so during family jam sessions. (Lila did this exactly once, and I almost lost my mind from pure joy. After that, she refused to ever play her part again.) My ideal is all about family harmony—literally and figuratively. Part of my own Good Mother Myth is this notion that because I am creative and musical, all my interactions with my kids should be full of these qualities, and that they should receive my instruction gratefully, sort of like the kids in the Partridge Family. I want to be Shirley Jones, beaming at her talented offspring, and once in a while humbly and sweetly singing a solo, somewhere off behind her keyboards.

Even before I had children, I always knew I wouldn't have the patience, talent, skills, or the economic freedom to stay at home. And as a musician and writer, giving up my work to invest in parenting 24/7 would have been tantamount to giving up breathing. I knew this about myself when I got pregnant, and as my first baby grew inside me, I told her that I would have to work sometimes, that my connection to the earth through my music and writing was necessary to keep me sane. A sane, happy mother is a good mother, I murmured to the growing mound under my fingers. Yet despite the trade-off—or perhaps because of it—I am not always a sane and happy mother. For example, as I try to squeeze in work time at home, I berate myself for the fact that instead of teaching my son to play the guitar, I am letting him watch a DVD of me playing guitar. Then there are the many Fridays when I leave the kids with their father and travel around the country with my heart and thoughts anchored back in Massachusetts, with them. I get on stage at 8:00 PM and wonder where Tom and Lila are in the latest Harry Potter book. What am I missing? I am missing both the bedtime story *and* my moment on stage to connect with the audience—my moment to sing the song I wrote; my moment to take in all the years of hard work and good fortune that got me to this stage?

And so I always feel that I am doing B minus work. I am always scurrying to catch up with professional emails, connecting with agents and management, communicating with the students who come to my writing retreats and music classes, and on the worst days, there is just too much: the song is half-written, the email inbox is stuffed, the computer is knocked off line, both kids are screaming at each other, and once again, all I have to serve them for dinner is a box of mac 'n' cheese.

I have never hit either child, and I never will. No matter. In my own mind, I may as well have. I think often of the passage from Jesus's sermon on the mount where he says, "I tell you this: anyone who is angry with a brother or sister is subject to judgment" (Matt. 5:21). Yes, of course: *our own.* I can judge myself very harshly for being angry with my kids. And yet, what I notice is that after anger explodes in my house, as it inevitably does (several times a day, by all four family members), there is a fairly predictable aftermath. The exploder will rage; in the case of the under ten crowd, the raging will be audible. Those over twenty tend to seethe silently after barking some version of something horrible their parents said that they swore they'd never utter. But either way, the exploder, at some point, apologizes to the explodee. "I'm sowwy, Lila." Or, "Sweetheart, I wish I hadn't raised my voice. Let's talk about why it isn't okay to climb up the doorframe in your dirty sneakers. And here, here's a sponge. Let's clean it up together." We might be champion yellers, but we are also champion apologizers. And after a fight, as every lover knows, the bond seems tighter. The laughter is stronger, and the hugs are sweeter. And so far, trust has been maintained.

What is good enough? This is a legitimate question in an era where every parental failing can be scrutinized by the grown child once she enters the Church of Psychotherapy, a church I frequent still. Parents who are emotionally unavailable can be judged through the same lens as parents who beat, abused, or abandoned their children. One day when my kids were both under the age of four, I was talking to a friend about some particularly egregious moral parental failing of mine, such as ignoring them while I made a newsletter on the computer, and my friend, who was the daughter of an unrecovered alcoholic said, "You know, I keep realizing over and over that the mother I got was exactly the mother I needed in order to get to the place I am now. I am so grateful for having my mother. I wouldn't trade her for anyone else's."

What's good enough? We don't get to know. We don't get to *judge*. But we do get to pledge every morning to do the best we can, love the biggest love we've got, pay as much attention as we can muster, given our inevitable lack of sleep and level of overwhelm. A good barometer is this: How much did I *enjoy* my children today? How much did my own heart fill up with love and gratitude? If I go to bed smiling at something my child did or said, secure in the knowledge that she is fed and clothed and warm and loved, I call it a good day.

In fact, I might even call myself a good mother.

ANOTHER WAY
TO END THE EVENING /
ANDIE FOX

aT LEAST ONCE A YEAR, I PACK UP my two children and we drive away from my job and the house and their father. We stay somewhere cheap and peaceful, in the company of other mothers and their children. Usually, we holiday near the water so we can entertain ourselves and the children outside, beyond doors and walls. Sometimes there is long-term planning behind these holidays and we spend half a year looking forward to the escape, while other trips are much more spontaneous. On one occasion, a couple of mothers, as bored with school holidays as I, invited me for an impromptu holiday—leaving that very day. We drove for an hour and a half to cabins by a quiet river and reveled in the liberation. I should be on the run from the law, given how quickly I can pack, even with a child and baby underfoot. On that holiday, we ate whatever meals we could assemble from the random ingredients we'd taken from our kitchen cupboards in the rush to escape. Our partners, back in the city, felt both envious of the spontaneity and grateful for the unexpected quiet evenings.

While it is the carefully planned holidays that have undoubtedly been the most successful—like the week we stayed in a shack on a small sand island and made gourmet picnic dinners to eat on the beach while we watched pods of dolphins frolic offshore—it is the impulsiveness of the impromptu holiday that appeals most to me. Because when was the last time I felt some risk in my family routine? When did I last find the day adventurous as a mother? When did I last feel like *myself*?

Something interesting happens on these holidays with other mothers. The boundaries between families collapse without the fathers there to keep them nuclear. The children roam from cabin to cabin. They eat together and sometimes sleep together. If I am lucky, one of the mothers will take my children with her into a shower and she will wash the salt and sand out of their hair for me while I find their towels. My children will come back to my cabin and tell me about the pimple on her bottom.

When it is working well, the older children look out for the younger children, although soon enough they get bored and distracted and I have to look for the toddler again. And then another mother calls out that she has him and I can stop worrying for a moment. If there are enough children in the group, they form and pull apart and reform during the course of the day in different play configurations with different leaders, sometimes in pairs and sometimes in big groups, like flocks of birds. There are few fights on days like this.

The mothers I holiday with are the relaxed types. I like to watch them for clues. I peer into their parenting frameworks and get small shocks of insight when I see them not fuss over something I react to;

I like knowing there are other ways to do this, the sense of possibility. But mothering will make even the most relaxed among us irritable at times. These holidays are tiring because sometimes there are as many as ten children between us. When we take them to swim in the sea, we walk as far as we can carry the youngest of them and very often that will be to a beach lacking lifeguards. Cheap accommodation is not central to amenities. We herd the children into the sea and then position ourselves around them so we can bunch them up tightly, like hunters circling prey. This way we can count them more easily, an activity that requires an almost painful level of concentration as they bob under and up through the waves, and then we nudge them up the beach every few minutes, away from the riptides they are slipping into.

The children draw with sticks on the sand, the toddler falls asleep in my lap, we find a wobbegong shark for them to see in the water, and they fight over jellyfish eggs, proving that it is possible to squabble over any limited resource, no matter how random. These days are unexpectedly perfect. I plan for a perfect day so often with my children, almost every day in fact, but I rarely pull them off. When they finally happen they are often stunningly simple. There is a sense of lost community in these holidays, and I wonder if there was a time when mothering was more like this. Are we simply rediscovering something mothers used to know?

But it is not all sharing and harmony. At some point each mother becomes exhausted by her own children's demands and sometimes this happens simultaneously. The day threatens to shatter and buckle under the weight of all the children suddenly being hungry at once, or when one after another they hurt themselves or lose their things. We cannot offer help to one another in these times, though we would like to, because each mother is frantically tending to her own children. The relief I pull from this moment is looking up and seeing that all mothers get as exasperated as I do, and raise their voices. You can feel the tension, and everyone is tempted to throw in the towel and call it a day right there. But if we push through this until the children are bathed and fed and quiet again, then we can sit together for a glass of wine. By the evening I am in a kind of awe at these mothers and the way they summon patient voices for the last of their children's needs. I have a gentle voice by then too, but I am not used to observing it from the outside and I always suspect my own voice is less sincere than theirs. After all that we have been through during the day, I think, *if only your husband could see you and your stamina.* He thinks you are on *holiday* with the children. We talk about him, too, at that time of night when the children are not listening. (I have not been away with my lesbian friends like this, and I wonder how we would choose which partner to leave behind and talk about in their absence; so yes, we *talk about men* on these holidays.)

We talk about the arguments and the failed attempts at sharing workloads fairly. And we talk about the sex and how you never really completely know your partner—even after all the intensity and tedium of parenting together, they are still a mystery. And we talk about how that "intensity and tedium" either fuses you closer together or drives you apart. Sometimes we talk about knowing you could leave if you had to, if he did something terrible or things got that bad for you and you needed to start over. When you have children with someone it can be difficult to remember that kind of courage, but you need to know it about yourself, and you feel that much closer to the courage when you are drinking a glass of wine with your women friends.

There are two ways to end the night. The first is here, and most of the mothers I holiday with do, in fact, end it at this point. The children are sleepy and we peel apart to get them to their beds and wash up the dishes and make goodnight phone calls to our partners. There may be one last glass of wine together afterwards—and on one occasion, we mothers sneaked out to lie on a blanket and look at the stars, leaving the children in their beds—but often we are too constrained by separate dwellings and the need to keep to some kind of schedule.

But there is another way to end the evening. I have this other old friend, and when we go on holiday together we often take the children out for a walk along the beach at ten at night because it is just such a beautiful night, and if they get the cuffs of their pajamas wet and drag sand into the beds, well what does it matter? The walk was lovely. On these walks we will have our best conversation of the entire day. It will happen at that very moment in the evening, and we could have missed it if we had surrendered to the night any earlier. Sometimes it will be the most rewarding conversation I have had in weeks.

It's times like these where the words of author and poet Adrienne Rich come to mind:

"This is what living with children could be—without school hours, fixed routines, naps, the conflict of being both mother and wife with no room for being simply, myself."

The quote comes from a larger anecdote Rich describes of holidaying alone with her young sons while her husband is working abroad. Without a sense of outside authority in her home, Rich discards one "rule" after another about what it takes to be a good mother, including bedtime and routine. Suddenly she finds mothering both pleasurable and compatible with a sense of self.

Rich wrote these observations back in 1976 in *Of Woman Born*. Her book was a refreshing and intelligent exploration of the institution of motherhood. Rich has, at times, been unfortunately divisive for feminism at large, but there is no diminishing her importance to the feminist motherhood movement. Her discovery back in the seventies that being a "bad mother" could actually make you a "happy mother," and that happy mothers are good for their children, should not have been news to me when I started my own journey into motherhood in 2005. But those sentiments of Rich's are as revolutionary today as they were then, more than forty years ago. Motherhood, as an institution, remains oppressive to women today—competitive, artificial, isolated, and individualistic.

While some mothers will find a kind of structure in routine to support the chaos of the demands of mothering, other mothers, many more I suspect, will find a kind of pleasure in the chaos that can be located only when routine is abandoned.

In the nights where my friend and I take our children out with us, talking under the moonlight, we do something revolutionary—we show our children their mothers kicking free of the shackles. For our daughters, the lesson is that they can be mothers one day and not "lose themselves"; and for our sons, we teach them that women freed from rules are women at their happiest.

CLIMBERS /
DEBORAH SIEGEL

SOME PEOPLE THINK HAVING TWINS makes you badass. "Twins? Wow. Hardcore." This is what people say to you. After a year or two of hearing it, you begin to believe it yourself. Until you meet someone more badass than yourself: The Triplet Mom.

I was shuttling my toddlers up the four flights of stairs to their preschool classroom, wondering why this world-class synagogue didn't have an elevator. I was tired, very tired, from another night of interrupted sleep. My daughter had cried from three to five that morning with toddler demands. When the alarm clock went off an hour later, I felt faceless. By the third flight of stairs, my legs were weighty, my eyelids heavy. Earlier in the year, the climb seemed nearly impossible because my son had wanted to be carried. Not today. All things considered, we were making good progress.

Coming up behind me were Triplet Mom and her nanny. Between

her kids and mine, we were half the class. I felt solidarity with this mother of three, the way I did with all parents of multiples, but thus far, she and I had said little more to each other than hello. I grabbed the moment in the stairwell to court her as a friend, desperate as I was for connection.

On many levels, I found her appealing. Maybe it was her nose ring, or her surprisingly Zen demeanor, or the way two of her three children held her hands as they marched up the stairs. What an amazing mother she must be.

That said, I'd harbored a love/hate thing for this woman I barely knew, ever since the first day of class when, during snack time, she pulled out bottled water and earth-friendly thermoses to complement the Annie's Organic Bunny crackers she brought for her triplets. My kids, along with the only other two children in the class, drank New York City tap water out of plastic cups and munched on the generic goldfish the school provided.

Maybe it wasn't solidarity I felt in my compulsion to reach out, after all. Maybe I needed to overcome my own petty jealousy and prove something to myself.

"How's it going this morning?" I asked, flashing my eyes her way for half a moment, afraid that one or both of my toddlers might plummet if I released my gaze from their climb.

"Tired. But then, I always am," she said lightly, as if it were no big deal.

"I know," I related. Her three were doing an amazing job with the stairs. I marveled at the way two of them weren't even holding the railing, just her hand. Their nanny was gently nudging along the third. I encouraged my two to hold the railing and keep their eyes ahead.

"So, are you home with them every day?" I asked, my default gesture at conversation. Having a similar or at least complementary work/life setup seemed to be my prerequisite for mommy friendship during those early days of working motherhood. You had to find times to get together for playdates when you were both available, and be willing to weather friendships through cancellations when work issues came up. But aside from logistics, I simply related to working moms more. I found comfort in struggles that paralleled my own.

Triplet Mom stared into the middle distance. She sighed audibly. "It's different with triplets," she said. "It takes two adults. All the time." Was that a note of condescension in her voice? There was clear emotion behind the statement. I wondered if she thought I was judging her for staying home with a fulltime nanny. Maybe I was. Maybe I was just like the female resident at the hospital who, when I was a young girl being prepped for eye surgery, asked what my mother did for a living. When I told her that my mother stayed at home with me, the resident responded, *Is that all?*

As we rounded the landing for the final set of stairs to the top floor, I wondered why she seemed defensive. And did her answer mean she was a fulltime stay-at-home mom? Did having three kids at once mean this woman, by necessity, had to sacrifice her career—even with the help of a partner *and* a nanny? I found this notion threatening, the prospect of having so many kids that you *couldn't* work. I was struggling to contribute to the family treasure and still be there for my kids, with just two. Suddenly, my part-time working arrangement felt like not enough and yet too much. I stumbled for a moment and tripped up a stair.

And then, the unthinkable almost happened. I lost my balance and righted myself by leaning on my daughter's shoulder. She buckled just slightly from the pressure. I stopped in my tracks, took a deep breath, and tried to steady myself and my teetering self-doubt.

As we entered the classroom, my thoughts shifted from comparative work/life arrangements to competitive childrearing. This program required a caregiver's presence, so Triplet Mom, her nanny, and I all followed the kids into the room. Two of the triplets started building a high tower. "Oh, so high! So high!" cooed Triplet Mom. My son and I were banging two cardboard blocks together. ("Can he stack six blocks?" his occupational therapist had asked me the other day. I lied and said he could stack three.) When it was circle time and the teacher, Michele, started reading a book about trains, my son started to scream. Circle time was not his thing. I took him out of the room. As we left, the triplets were busy calling out different kinds of freight cars—"Flatcar!" "Hopper car!"

I paced the hallway, cradling my son in my arms, and prayed that he'd stop screaming. As soon as he stopped crying, I started crying myself. When we both finished, we returned to the room.

Mercifully, class eventually ended. I took a swig from my son's sippy cup and did a half-assed job wiping up some water I had spilled on the table, while trying to also keep an eye on my daughter and shove my son's arm into his jacket. My son started howling again as Michele handed out our kids' artwork from last week. Triplet Mom laid her kids' paintings on the table near me, where I had spilled the water, and where I continued to wrangle children and water and coats. "Excuse me," she said, maneuvering the pictures out from under my coat, where they lay dangerously close to the pool of water. "Ohhh, *water*," she said, disappointedly. *Yes, water!* I wanted to say. *NON-ORGANIC WET WATER ON YOUR TRIPLETS' ART!* I sucked in my breath instead and led my twins back down the stairs.

Later that morning, while pushing my kids home in their stroller, I found myself wondering about the intensity of my emotion and self-doubt. Why did I judge myself so fiercely? Why did I judge other mothers, in spite of my need to connect? While I found comfort in struggles that paralleled mine, the flipside was also true. I felt distanced by differences. The gulf seemed to widen whenever somebody mentioned full-time help.

As I bumped the stroller down the three stairs leading to our ground floor apartment, I realized that in my mental replay, I had muted a key tidbit of the conversation with Triplet Mom. Somewhere between the third and fourth flights, before we'd reached the classroom, she had asked if *I* worked. I told her yes, part-time and largely from home. She said that seemed like the ideal. Once her kids were a bit older, she hoped maybe she'd be able to work again, too. We were sisters in work/life struggle, and all I could focus on in that moment was who was getting it "right."

About a year earlier, just as my twins were starting to sit up, *The New York Times* ran a forum about "competitive mothering" featuring prominent novelists and memoirists, an anthropologist, a historian of childrearing practices, an editor, and an entrepreneur. The forum was titled, "Who's the Best Mommy of Them All?" When the kids went down for their nap the next day, I pulled that forum up online, took a second look, and jotted down some gems in the Moleskine notebook I kept stuffed in my diaper bag, a remnant of my pre-motherhood self.

"Moms worry for a living," wrote British novelist Allison Pearson. "If we screw up our job, it's not a delivery of fruit that goes bad. It's the next generation."

"It's as though our identities are on the line with decisions about the permissibility of dessert," added Judith Warner, author of *Perfect Madness: Motherhood in the Age of Anxiety*. She dispensed salient wisdom about the contexts in which our criticisms take place:

"Our much-vaunted 'choices,' in an absence of family-friendly social policies, have largely proven hollow. For most mothers, the real freedom to choose how they live their lives remains a distant dream. Many blame themselves for falling short and then buttress themselves against self-criticism by critiquing other mothers' so-called choices."

Hollow. Real freedom. Distant dream. So-called choices. The words softened me enough to open my heart to what Triplet Mom's reality might possibly be.

I wish I could report that we grew better acquainted over coffee. In reality, I Googled her. And in the blue haze of isolation, up late one night while the rest of my family slept, I learned that both Triplet Mom and her husband were filmmakers. Her husband had recently premiered a documentary about technology that featured their kids as newborns. I watched the online trailer. Actually, I watched it three times, taking in the miraculous images of three bug-eyed newborns with scrawny fingers and blue-tinged skin. I learned something profound about the triplets' beginnings. Born too early, they lived in neonatal intensive care, dependent on machines, for the first several months of their lives. In the film, the babies had oxygen tubes tucked under their tiny noses and EKG wires running every which way along their delicate chests. In one still image, the forefinger of an adult hand caressed a forehead through an incubator. The infant's entire head was no larger than a fist.

I learned something about their first few months at home. Once released from the hospital, their parents were cautioned to limit their exposure to any germs or viruses, lest they end up back in intensive care. Were I in Triplet Mom's place, I too might have monitored their intake down to their Annie's bunny crackers. And I sure as hell would have found a way to have two adults at home. All the time. No matter what it might take.

About a year later, I had a second perspective-altering experience, one that flattened me with all the subtlety of a freight train's engine car. This time, it was even more humbling than before.

I was sitting in the community room with my husband in a circle of parents at my twins' new preschool. We had moved across the country to be closer to family. The room was named for a child who had died of cancer when he was five years old. It was the inaugural meeting of the school's Inclusion Support Group, a monthly gathering of parents with children who had special needs of varying order, led by the school's Director of Child Development. My son had some sensory issues that raised flags and landed him an aide in the school's inclusion program. We were still figuring out what he needed, but most of the others parents had kids who were autistic, and more.

Real freedom. Distant dream. So-called choices. The words came back to me in this sober setting, waking me to the reality that, depending on the hand we are dealt, parenthood can be nothing like what we expect it will be.

Some children are in need of special protection. Those needs are frequently invisible from the perch on which other parents sit and judge. Other times, our judgment of parents assumes a need for correctness or control on their part, when in reality, as in the case of Triplet Mom, they might very well be acting on fears based on harrowing experiences. Or they might simply be making different choices. Organic ones.

I'd like to report that with the passage of time, I've grown less judgmental—that I now practice sisterly motherhood, and motherly sisterhood. For the most part, I do—or rather, I try. And certainly, there is more room for empathy now that my toddlers are sleeping through most of the night.

There remain times, of course, when I revert to my old ways of thinking. At those moments, I hear the familiar cadence chugging down the track: *Am I good enough? Am I doing this right? Are my children developing on target? Do I work too much? Not enough? Don't I care?*

The scripts inside our heads are relentless. The scripts are insidious. I want what all good mothers want: healthy and happy kids, with room for myself in the mix. With all the energy I spend locked in judgment, I could organize a stroller brigade. When I default to my old ways, I often find myself thinking how very different life might be if all of us good mothers realized the extent to which our climbs up the stairs were shared. If I were to meet Triplet Mom on the stairs again, if I could say one thing to her, I hope it would be: *Wow, sister. What an amazing mother you are.*

IS THIS MOTHERHOOD OR MIDDLE SCHOOL? /
NAOMI SHULMAN

a COUPLE OF MONTHS AGO, I RAN INTO Sandy, a woman who used to be a fixture in my everyday life—our kids were in the same toddler playgroup. We never really clicked, but having bumped into each other at a lecture by a local speaker, it would have been socially awkward not to say hi. We fell into polite conversation: *How are you? Fine, and you? Fine.*

Then things veered off script.

"Naomi, I think of you every Sunday night!" Sandy put in suddenly.

"Really?" I replied.

"You know *Downton Abbey?*" she asked, breaking into a wide, toothy smile. "You look just like Lady Edith!"

Crash course on *Downton Abbey*: Lady Edith is the middle of three daughters—the ugly one. With her overbite, weak chin, and rounded shoulders, her homeliness is actually a major plot point. Put bluntly: She's a dog. (And, no, I *don't* look like her.)

Which is why I immediately responded, somewhat incredulously, "You mean the *homely* one?"

Sandy's expression didn't change. "Oh, *I* don't think she's homely," she insisted. And then the irony overwhelmed me, because the lecture Sandy and I had *just* sat through for the past hour was all about female social aggression. Rachel Simmons, author of *Odd Girl Out* and *Curse of the Good Girl*, had just finished describing the way tween girls wield power by making snide comments, and then accusing the victim of being oversensitive. Simmons kept her talk confined to middle schoolers, but here we were, two grown women, acting out a page from one of her books.

A lot of research on female social aggression focuses on middle school because that's when things tend to get out of hand. We parents anxiously watch over our daughters (and to some extent our sons) as they navigate the shark-infested waters of junior high school, praying they will emerge unscathed. But a woman of any age likely has a recent anecdote of girl-on-girl social swordplay. Some studies have shown that relational aggression can start in preschool, and it continues all the way to the nursing home, where old biddies pull the same crap one might expect of their great-granddaughters. ("What happens to mean girls? Some of them go on to become mean old ladies," quipped one nursing home aide to *The New York Times* in 2011.) Middle school is the classic zenith, but I think there's another time when social aggression ramps up: early motherhood.

Disclaimer: I am not a social scientist and I have no research to back this up. I do, however, have eyes. Think about it—new mothers are overwhelmed with hormones; our changing bodies feel unfamiliar and weird. We are entering a world of high stakes, and we are often scared. Remind you of anything? Just as in middle school, new parenthood is a time when many of us seek out new friends, not only to relieve the monotony of childcare but also to validate our choices and bolster our insecurities. Tween girls list their friendships as the most important element in their lives, which is why the threat of losing a friend—or worse, being cut off from a *group* of friends—is such a potent threat at that age. As women mature, we still have close friendships, but we aren't so deeply invested in them—we focus on career, on dating, on building our lives. Once we get pregnant, however, many of us turn again to our peers—sometimes with the same results we had the last time around.

We operate under the illusion that we have all that social noise under control. Decent moms—decent *women*—are too mature, too socially evolved, to get all seventh-grade on each other (or, at the very least, too busy). But it was in the throes of new parenthood that I was last dumped, painfully and inexplicably, by a friend I'd made in a postpartum support class. Lonely and freaked out by motherhood, with my marriage rocking at least as precipitously as the proverbial cradle, I leaned on my new mom friendships harder than I had since—well, since I was about twelve. This new friend and I bonded quickly and deeply. It was about cracked nipples and sleep deprivation and rice cereal, yes—but not really. It was *really* over our sudden transformation from hip young chicks to frazzled young mothers, and over the space of just a few weeks, she became something like a best friend. We managed to get out to the park several times a week; we met for coffee and lunch at relaxed eateries, strollers in tow; we were on the phone pretty much every day, comparing notes about pediatrician visits, laundry pileups, the milestones our babies were hitting.

And looking back, maybe that was part of the problem. We weren't just comparing notes; we were *comparing*, period. *How much weight did you gain? How much have you lost? How much milk are you producing? Oh, your baby isn't sitting up yet? Hm.* In the attempt to mask our insecurities, even the most grown-up of us fall prey to some seriously immature behavior. I began to sense that my parenting style wasn't cool enough for my new-mommy friend. When she dumped me, she did it just the way my middle school frenemies had, decades prior: She gave me the silent treatment. My calls and emails went unreturned; I found myself holding my baby in the park, alone.

We see this writ large in national conversations—hello, Mommy Wars! It's reflected in our books (*Bringing Up Bebe*, *The Battle Hymn of the Tiger Mother*), our movies (*I Don't Know How She Does It*). Read the comments at many online parenting sites and you'll get a strong whiff of junior high. The minute a woman becomes pregnant, every choice she makes, from what she eats to where the baby sleeps to whether she works or stays home, becomes fodder for other mothers to analyze and judge. It is distressingly similar to walking through the halls of your local middle school, feeling critical eyes upon you, hearing the hushed murmurs of other girls making their cruel assessments. Most of those girls feel the same way when *they* walk through the halls. That's the point: We judge others to deflect the risk of being judged. And now we're expected to model healthy interpersonal behavior for our kids.

There's a flip side, though. Being so invested in my friendships wasn't all pain; most days, meeting up with my mom posse was a balm. We congregated at child-friendly cafes, the ones that had train tables in the back, and huddled over our lattes, trading stories and support. That woman who dumped me? She was an aberration. By the time my first child was toilet trained and I was pregnant with my second, I was comfortably ensconced in a strong circle of friends—maybe ten of us—with kids the same ages; we met at the family drop-in center several days a week. Every time I walked into the family center, I felt like Norm in *Cheers*—everyone knew me, I knew everyone, and my grown-up self relaxed into the social stew. I was so enamored with the family center, in fact, that I joined the board.

And it was during a board meeting that the director of the family center brought up a touchy subject. "It seems that some of the new moms coming to visit find this place kind of, um, cliquey," she said.

"Really? That's weird," I said immediately. *I* had never felt anything but the warmth and ease of total acceptance. "Who said that?"

"Well, I can't name names," the director continued. "But, Naomi . . . I think some of them think you and your friends actually *are* one of those cliques."

"That's crazy," I responded. And then the room fell silent. I heard someone clear their throat.

Could it be true? Anyone who went to middle school with me can tell you I was the *furthest* thing from a cool kid; I was always a little nerdy, a little clueless. But I had to admit, I didn't feel nerdy or clueless anymore. I felt . . . popular. I wasn't actively excluding anyone! I just didn't have time to be friends with everyone. But is that how it felt to them?

More to the point, is that how it felt to Sandy, the lady of the *Downton Abbey* comment? Because, as I mentioned, that's how we first knew each other—seeing one another across the room at the family center, day after day. Did she resent me? Is that why, even years after the onslaught of new motherhood was behind us, we still related to each other with all the wariness and mistrust of middle schoolers?

After that incident at the lecture, I immediately turned to my husband and, yes, my closest friends, who reassured me that I did *not* look like Lady Edith (as if!) and confirmed my suspicions that Sandy was just being snarky. But I don't know if it's that simple. The next day I got a Facebook message from Sandy. "I just wanted to say it was lovely to see you at such a great event last night," she wrote, ". . . and to let you know that I think you're quite fetching."

She'd clearly been thinking about the incident as well, and while she didn't exactly apologize for the slight, she was aware that what she said made me feel bad. Should I have pressed her to acknowledge the put-down, and let her know I took it personally? Should I have not responded at all, giving her the Facebook equivalent of the silent treatment?

I may have taken one of those courses of action thirty years ago, but I am not actually twelve anymore. I know I have hurt people's feelings myself (maybe Sandy's, in fact), and I know we're all just doing the best we can with the resources we have. And as mothers—adult women who have the power to nurture instead of negate—I like to think we are kinder, more empathetic beings for it, and Sandy's follow-up message was an example of that. Most importantly, I am my daughters' first role model in how women relate to other women. So I reread her message, took a deep breath, and wrote back simply, "Thanks, Sandy! It was nice to see you too." And then I clicked *send*.

THERE'S A ZOMBIE CAVEWOMAN IN ALL OF US /
AMBER DUSICK

I WAS SHOPPING AT TRADER JOE'S WITH my two boys, a nine-month-old and a three-year-old. We were out of toothpaste at home, so against my better judgment, I forced myself to go to the market with them. It was the lesser of two evils: risk of cavities and all-but-certain bad breath, or possibility of in-store tantrum. I'd take that latter challenge.

Honestly, I dreaded taking my children places at that age. It was almost always a disaster. Plus, I hadn't had a good night's sleep in months, and I felt and looked like a zombie—albeit one with children in tow. But since I only planned to grab a couple of things, I figured we'd get in and out in a jiffy. No problem! I told myself.

Right.

After only a few minutes in the grocery store, my nine-month-old started getting antsy in the cart and my three-year-old was asking for a cereal bar he'd seen several aisles back. I did *not* want to go back for it. I was on a mission. Get toothpaste and get *out*. But I made the mistake of slowing down to think about this decision rather than simply maintain the cart's pace. It was only a split second, but toddlers can detect parental weakness. And that's when they pounce. Sensing my hesitation, he ran off to find the cereal bar himself. *Urghhh*. Frustrated, I followed him.

"Wait!" I whisper-yelled, "That isn't the right *aisle!*"

He turned the corner sharply and barrelled face-first into a woman's cart. *Sigh*. He started crying—loudly and uncontrollably. I knelt down and held him in my arms as he wailed. Hearing his brother cry, my nine-month-old son burst into tears too.

It felt like the entire store froze into statues around us—statues with disapproving looks on their faces.

I saw what they saw: a frazzled mother with dirty hair pulled into a haphazard ponytail wearing yoga pants and a ratty old t-shirt, and two crying kids with stained shirts, tangled hair, and food on their faces. Oh, and stinky breath. We looked and probably smelled more Neanderthal than Homo sapien. I had to get us out of there. Should I ditch the cart? No, that would be even more embarrassing. I had to do what was necessary to salvage my last vestige of dignity. *Just grab the cereal bars, pay, and leave.* We could survive three more minutes. No problem!

As we rushed to the checkout, I saw her. I noticed her shoes first. To-die-for aqua peep toe heels with white trim. She had makeup on and her hair looked like she'd just left a salon. She was wearing accessories. *Accessories!* I had forgotten about the existence of accessories. I was quite sure this woman only wore yoga pants to actually *do* yoga. She was totally on top of things. And she was a mother of young children. Indeed, she had a child just a little older than my youngest in her cart and another child just a little older than my eldest walking beside her. Her kids were calm and clean and happy. She lazily pushed her cart, taking time to read labels on yogurt.

I imagined going up to her, shaking her by the shoulders and demanding, "How do you do this?! How do you make it look so easy?!" Maybe touching her would have revealed that she was actually a robot. *Oh my god, Stepford Wives DO exist!* It would be much easier to believe she wasn't real, otherwise I was a complete and utter failure at this motherhood gig. It sure felt like it in that moment.

We made it through the checkout line—kids still wailing, me with a tight smile as I tossed cash on the counter—and into the parking lot. RELIEF! But as I buckled the kids into their car seats, my heart sank—pretty much all the way down to my vagina, and then easily fell out on to the seat of the car. I had forgotten the toothpaste! It was the whole reason we'd come to the market. I couldn't even manage to buy toothpaste for my family.

It was official, I was a complete and utter failure. With bad breath.

I cried the whole drive home.

This was one of the lowest periods of my parenting career. While I'm not one to compare myself to others, I just couldn't let go of that peep-toe-heeled mom. Over the next few days, I thought about her. More honestly, I *obsessed* over her. How much time did it take her to get ready each day? How clean was her house? I bet she had a nanny! Did *she* ever forget to buy toothpaste? Were her kids calm and happy because of the way that she parented? Wait—was I somehow screwing up my kids? What was I doing wrong? Why was this so *hard* for me?

A few months went by and this darkness lifted. I was amazed by what a few hours of uninterrupted sleep could do for a person. I felt almost human again.

One afternoon, I was at Target with both kids. But I wasn't wearing yoga pants. I had on a skirt. And a necklace. Yes, *accessories.* I was also wearing makeup, and while my hair never looks like I just left a salon (including when I actually have just left a salon), I looked and felt great. My kids were being unusually mellow as I pushed the cart down the aisles.

We had evolved.

But I didn't notice this difference until I saw *her*. A stressed-out and disheveled ponytail mom with a screaming baby in her cart. She looked fragile. I could tell she was hanging by a thread. I could tell because I've hung by it many times myself. I felt her eyes on us as we walked by.

For the first time in months, I thought of the mom in the peep toe heels. It felt like an entire lifetime had gone by. Now *I* was the one breezing past making it all look simple. Did the ponytail mom wonder how I did it? The thought of this seemed ridiculous. I couldn't imagine someone looking at me and thinking I had it all together. It made me sad to think that it could actually make her feel worse. What if she obsessed over me like I'd obsessed over the peep–toe–heeled mom?

I wanted to reach out and tell her that it was hard for me too. That I am not a robot Stepford Wife. I wanted to reassure her that it would get easier. Sorta. That it wouldn't always be this difficult or this tiring. That she wouldn't always look and feel like a zombie—or a Neanderthal, depending on the day. Why? Because nobody is perfect all of the time —or actually ever. I wanted to tell her to be gentle with herself. To assure her that, yes, she is having a difficult time right now, but it doesn't define her. She is *not* a failure.

I watched as the ponytail mom abandoned her cart and carried her baby out of the store. She was gone before I ever had the courage to approach her. But it didn't really matter. Those messages weren't just for her. They were for me.

I will never be the peep–toe–heeled mom, because she doesn't exist. Sure, I saw that mom in Trader Joe's, but I knew nothing about her. Perhaps she hung from a thread on her off days, too. I'm willing to bet she's actually a lot like me, just with better shoes.

Even when I get a full night of sleep and I'm wearing a skirt and my kids are mellow, I will always have that frazzled mom-in-yoga-pants zombie cavewoman inside of me. I've accepted her. And I'm gentle with her.

Even when she forgets stuff at the market.

NO MORE FAKEBOOK /
SARAH EMILY TUTTLE-SINGER

S O, ACCORDING TO FACEBOOK, this is how I spent my Saturday with the kids:

My children and I woke up with the sun, smiling and ready to kick ass and "make it a great day." My hair was shiny. My smile, too. We drank our morning drinks in latte cups—frothy foam mustaches lacing our lips. We played backgammon, our skin mottled by drops of shade in the morning light. We went for a walk in the orchards, and we danced between emerald leaves like fairies. We rocked out to Red Hot Chili Peppers.

'Cuz that's how we roll: Just another day being totally awesome. And while all of this is basically true, I'm also full of shit. Here's how it really went down.

My children and I did wake up with the sun. Waaaay too early because *someone* forgot to close the blinds the night before. Sure, they were smiling and ready to kick ass and "make it a great day."

I wasn't.

But hey, I had enough stamina to trudge out of bed, turn on the TV, power up the DVD player, and press play. I didn't even bother to rub the crap from my eyes. By the time Belle finished bitching and moaning about her "provincial life," I was asleep. I dreamed there was a dog kissing my face. I batted it away. I heard my daughter scream "DON'T HIT ME, MAMA!" I opened my eyes: My daughter was the dog. And it was clearly time to brush teeth, because—oops!—we crashed hard the night before and Mama of the Year may have let the nighttime ritual slide.

So we brushed our teeth and took turns peeing.

"Mama, why does your vagina have a tail?"

Huh?

"Oh, that's a tampon."

"What's a tampon?"

(Once upon a time when I used to read books on parenting—before I had kids—I learned that when it comes to tricky questions about where babies come from, you should only answer the specific question asked. Think hostile witness on the stand and get serious.)

"Tampons go inside your vagina."

"Why?"

"Because they stop the blood from coming out of your vagina."

My kids took it all in stride.

"Why do you have blood in your vagina?"

Oy.

"Every month if there isn't a baby in my uterus, I have blood. It doesn't hurt, and the tampon stops it from getting in my underwear."

"I want a tampon," my son said. I gave him a clean one. He unwrapped it, grabbed the string, and hit his sister on the ear.

We ate leftover schnitzel and chocolate cake. Breakfast of champions, people. And I took several "spontaneous" pictures of all of us smiling with a camera timer. ("Come on . . . *Please.* Smile, dammit! Look happy!")

The kids went back to the TV, and I hit up Facebook to see what everyone else was doing. Most of my Facebook friends with kids were telling their Saturday stories for the world to "like." Homegirl posted a picture of her and her brood frolicking in a field of red poppies. (And I felt a twinge of envy.)

I clicked "like."

Another friend wrote, "My hubby makes the best pancakes for our little man." (And I threw up a little in my mouth.)

I also clicked "like."

And not to be outdone, I uploaded our new pictures. "Sunny Saturday!" I wrote in the status. I'm not a total liar. I'm just good at PR.

Time passed—five minutes? An hour? When you're blissfully ignoring your kids, the seconds slip by far too quickly.

We were on the third cycle of *Beauty and the Beast* when the Internet went out. I started to shake. I couldn't breathe. My window to the outside world was shuttered and locked.

"What about the Internet on your phone?" you ask. Well, let me tell it to you. I live in the middle of nowhere. And my 3G network prefers chillin' in cafes in Tel Aviv—sure, I understand, I'm the same way. But it still sucks.

Because, guess what? Now I have to actually spend my entire weekend with the kids; actually *with* the kids.

And here's the dirty little secret that I'll never admit on Facebook: I love my kids every freaking second. Would I die for them? You bet. Would I kill for them? Hurt my child, and I will cut you. But I don't always want to be with them.

Oh, and meanwhile? We were also out of coffee.

So we got dressed. I squeezed into a pair of Spanx—because three years postpartum, there are days when I still look pregnant. My belly is soft and mushy, and when I'm naked, I love how it feels between my fingers. But a muffin top is still a muffin top, so I tucked my Spanx into my bra, pulled on my skinny jeans, put on a red tank top, and zipped up my hooker boots.

Always my hooker boots, people. Both online and "IRL."

Meanwhile, my son wanted to wear his sister's dress, but she didn't want him to wear her dress. She shouted that penises don't wear dresses. He screamed that penises do wear dresses.

"Do not!"

"Do too! Mama, can penises wear dresses?" my son asked.

"Sure they can. But, Dude, that's your sister's dress, so the two of you need to work it out."

There was a thud. Then silence. Then she screamed. Then he screamed. And FYI? I was in the bathroom the whole time covering my zits and flat ironing my hair, and so I'm really not sure who pushed who first.

I came out screaming.

"What the hell is going on? Get dressed! You're wearing this! You're wearing that! Get your asses in gear, right now." I clapped my hands like a drill sergeant and counted down. "Chop chop. Ten, nine, eight . . . " People, when you're parenting solo and your Internet is out and you wanna get coffee, you do what works. And believe you me, this method works.

I can go on, but you get the idea.

Yes, we did drink out of oversized coffee mugs. But my son spilled his hot chocolate all over the floor.

Yes, we did play backgammon—but by "play backgammon" I really mean we built towers out of the backgammon chips for a grand total of two minutes and thirty-three seconds before my daughter realized that two of the white pieces were missing and her tower would never be as big as her brother's.

Yes, we went for a walk in the orchards. But within minutes, we were soaked in mud and our feet were cold. And both kids were whining because the clementine juice stung their fingers.

Yes, we rocked out to Red Hot Chili Peppers. But just one song before my kids took the CD player hostage and put on a Disney singalong. FML, people. FML.

Yes, there were blissful moments on that Saturday with my kids—moments I quickly captured in photographs and Facebook statuses, like butterflies pinioned to a board. "Look everyone! Look! My kids are happy! I'm happy! *We're happy!*"

And yes, we *are* happy. Most of the time. But there are times when we aren't. And by only sharing the cute and cuddly moments, I ignore the importance of the raw and the real hours that are spent in the trenches making mistakes and learning from them. For instance:

* Close the damn shades at night, or expect to be woken up at an unholy hour.
* Make your children brush their teeth, or they will have dog breath.
* If you're on the rag, maybe change your feminine hygiene products alone with the door closed. And locked.
* Always know your neighbor's Internet code in case of an emergency.

And instead of pretending that everything is hunky-freaking-dory, let's be real: Parenting is ridiculously hard. And all of us do ourselves and each other a huge disservice when we pretend otherwise. Sure, there are great times that should be celebrated. Sure, when our kids do awesome things, by all means, let's get our brag on. But let's also not tell each other so many lies by omission.

My life on Facebook is an airbrushed and Instagrammed image of my real life. I edit the suckage because I want people to think I have my shit together. I give everything a hiptacular filter to make the drudgery look interesting. Most of the time, I think I'm a decent mom, and I think I'm giving my kids a pretty good life. But I also think I'd be a better mom if I stopped pretending, and making friends on Facebook feel like they have to pretend as well.

Keeping up with the status messages is exhausting. And it turns friends into frenemies.

Anyway . . .

For all the lies of omission I've told on Facebook, I'm sorry. I'm really, really, really sorry. I can't promise that I won't do it again, but I can promise that I'll try to be more real. For all of our sakes.

Because here's the deal: Parts of my Saturday sucked big time. And I'm telling you this because I bet parts of your Saturday sucked big time as well. And if that's the case, I want you to know that all my shiny, happy, status messages aside, I get it. And if you want to talk about parenting with me—like, really break it down so we can rebuild—I'm here.

Reprinted courtesy of Kveller.com, where it originally appeared on February 25, 2013.

OH FATHER, WHERE ART THOU? / LISA DUGGAN

I SAT IN THE GLIDER NURSING MY two-month-old daughter. From the living room I could hear the sounds of my husband and mother watching TV together and laughing.

"Hey," I called out, "can someone give me a hand . . . *Hello?*"

Immobilized by my nursing-pillow contraption and a newborn infant asleep on my lap, there was no way to get up without waking the baby unless I passed her to someone else. My bladder was painfully full and my feet had fallen asleep. No one came, no one even answered. I had never felt so alone in my life, and I remember thinking: *So this is motherhood.*

Eventually, Mom's two-week stay ended, Frank went back to work, and it was just Alice, me, and the cats. Sure, there was an endless rotation of friends and family coming to see the baby, but no new mother next door to commiserate over coffee with. I became so grateful for my husband's company in the ten minutes before his bus came that I once thanked him endlessly for a bowl of cut-up bananas and raisins that he'd prepared for my breakfast. "You know," he said, on his way out the door, "that's what they give monkeys in cages."

Oh, I thought, *what I wouldn't give to be the most popular exhibit at the zoo!*

The first time I heard the phrase "stay-at-home mother," I pictured my husband leaving for work, followed eagerly down the sidewalk by me: "Lisa! Staaay . . . stay . . . good girl!" I never imagined my humorous vision would come true, and that Frank would indeed do the leaving, every day, and me the staying put. What I would eventually discover, during my at-home tenure, was this scene repeated all over the neighborhood. The dads left. The moms stayed.

In my early days of motherhood, I would often go hours without uttering a single recognizable word or hearing another adult's voice— save that of my husband's when he returned home at seven in the evening. I *cooed*. I *shushed*. I *hummed*. I rushed to the door when the mail hit the slot and cornered the mailman, eager for some human interaction that did not require me lifting my shirt. If it weren't for my weekly "mother-infant circle" at the lactation center in Chatham, New Jersey, I might have lost the use of language altogether.

The compassion and good advice I found at the center gave me the courage to keep going on the worst of days. Here, women felt free to tearfully recount stories of greedy all-night nursers or insensitive husbands. Here, I felt safe enough to expose any fears or doubts about my daughter's development, or my own ability to parent, knowing I would find sympathy in the circle around me. But we couldn't remain members there forever. We evolved into a rotating playgroup, meeting at one another's houses every Wednesday.

Somehow I found myself the member of a second playgroup as well, this one comprised of a small trio of moms I knew from my birthing classes. We met every other Friday. In both cases, I felt lucky to have been invited to join. When you're a thirty-seven-year-old new mother, making new friends isn't always easy and not something I was told to expect when I was expecting—along with the hemorrhoids and stretch marks.

Both groups were made up of intelligent, funny, and educated women in their middle to late thirties, all of whom had left full-time careers to have kids. All owned beautiful homes in leafy, suburban, New Jersey towns. Everyone served a nice spread when it was their turn to host. But they were different in a few ways. The moms in the bigger group had decided to remain stay-at-home moms and were devoted to increasing their family size, while the moms in the smaller Friday group all eventually went back to full-time careers.

Regardless of what choice they made, these women all had one thing in common: their husbands had careers, and with the exception of one dad, they played only a minor role in the domestic realm.

Despite this, I considered the mothers in both groups to be feminists—even if they didn't self-identify as such—because independent of their husbands, they were in charge of their lives and their choices, and each one seemed fiercely committed to her chosen path. They made clear that although their husbands' input on the care and raising of the kids was desired and solicited, it was the mothers who made the majority of the day-to-day decisions—and their husbands preferred it that way. As a freelance graphic designer, doing project-based work, I straddled the fence of these two distinct worlds: the stay-at-homers and the full-time working moms, but the grass seemed perpetually greener on both sides of that fence.

When I was working, I was thinking about my daughter. I missed her sweet baby smell. I missed the languid rhythm of a day spent focused on meeting her needs. When I was at home, I was thinking of work; specifically, an air-conditioned office with other adults, the frenetic rhythm of meeting a deadline, and the luxury of meeting my own needs first. No matter which job I was doing, at the end of the day, the only thing I was certain about was my ambivalence.

It was easy to diagnose my dissatisfaction as the popular and virally enhanced Mommy Wars: Who does it better, the stay-at-homers or the working mommas? The media pitted us against each other and further confounded our choices. We were damned if we did, and damned if we didn't. Either way, we were apparently screwing up our children.

Something was missing from these discussions, but I couldn't articulate what it was at first. The problem seemed unnameable, which added to my sense of isolation and transported me right back to Betty Friedan's pre-*Mystique* days. Eventually, I began to see that it was not a *something* that was missing, but a *someone*. Specifically, a man—and men in general.

Where the hell had all the men gone?

Yes, it's true, more daddies are home taking care of the kids today than any generation before ours. But take a walk around my neighborhood and you'd never guess this to be the case. At the grocery store or at school, on the playground or in the doctor's office, I'm usually surrounded by other women—and that includes the hired help. Our local librarian once described this phenomenon to me as "entering mommy-world," where children are passed from one pair of female hands to another, all day long.

As a feminist, you'd think I would have enjoyed this long soak in estrogen, but this one-gendered world felt alien and lopsided to me. Before I became a mother I had been working in corporate America for seventeen years, alongside both women and men. I didn't know that having a kid meant moving out of an integrated office to some oddly segregated suburb, or leaving half the population behind. I felt demoted. I felt *un*liberated. I felt like I had been sent back in time to sit at the kid's table.

My uncertainty about choosing to stay home was influenced by the fact that none of my male colleagues had made the same choice when they became parents; that, and the gap that began to form between my husband's daily life and mine. He was still living his old, pre-child life, with only minor adjustments. He could work late without giving a thought to who would watch our daughter. He had time to read the paper, talk on the phone, drink coffee while it was still hot. He had at least a train-ride-home amount of time to just sit and think. And he continued to develop his professional skills—and be compensated for them—while my skills withered away and my Social Security earnings chart turned into an inverted pyramid.

The public conversations about parenthood reinforce this ancient separation between men and women, too. It's still mothers who star in laundry detergent commercials, and reality shows swap moms, not dads. In the blogs I read, and in even the most progressive of newspapers, men and fathers are conspicuously absent from the dialogue—largely because no one thinks to ask them how *they* are combining parenthood and work. If I relied on these media images alone, I might conclude that taking care of babies and kids is still solely a woman's job, no matter if she is permanently parked at home or out pulling down a breadwinning salary.

Missing my male colleagues, I actively sought out stay-at-home fathers in my community and in my work as a writer and publisher. In 2011, I even went so far as to attend the sixteenth annual At-Home Dads Convention in Washington, D.C. (Yes, the *sixteenth year!* I never knew there were enough stay-at-home dads to make a convention from, let alone for sixteen years in a row.)

I went not only as a journalist but also as a participant—the first woman to have ever paid to attend. I learned from these pioneering papas that despite their many years staying-at-home, no one was celebrating their presence, let alone throwing them a shower. Despite being proud to do the traditional job of homemaker, they are reluctant to announce themselves as such. In fact, among the at-home dad tribe, when a father chooses to declare himself the stay-at-home parent to all his friends and family, it's called "coming out of the pantry."

If men are ashamed to embrace the title and work I specifically stayed home to do, what does that say about its value to the world? What is the point of fighting the Mommy Wars when no one values the spoils? Why do we keep re-enlisting to battle only among ourselves?

As my daughter grew up, I met more stay-at-home dads and it definitely eased my fear of being doomed by biological determinism. My world began to feel more in balance. Befriending fathers also forced me to face my own sexist thinking. I had to consciously reject what my unconscious mind had concluded about women's dominant presence at home: that women were better suited to parenthood. Working side-by-side with these fathers also helped me to see and appreciate the emotional depth of men. I always knew women were capable of being ambitious, competitive, and financially successful—qualities traditionally considered masculine. To me, it was a revelation that a dad could know his children as well, and care as deeply for them, as a woman could.

I think we are a ways off from seeing playgrounds integrated as equally by gender as our work-spaces are becoming, but we are headed positively in that direction. My hope is that the myth of the Good Mother will collapse under the weight of the mounting evidence that you no longer need to be either perfect—or even female—to properly nurture children.

My daughter turns ten this year. I recently asked her opinion on who was more suited for taking care of kids, men or women? "Well, mom," she said, "it involves both science and who's doing the work. If men start doing it more, eventually it will become part of their DNA."

I think Alice is right. We could end the Mommy Wars by the next generation, if we would only call in the fathers for reinforcement.

PART III

INSIDE MAMA'S MIND

AN EXISTENTIAL CRISIS IS BORN /
ALY WINDSOR

FTER MY FIRST CHILD WAS BORN, I became obsessed with death. Witnessing life begin made me think about how and when and where it might end. It made me think of my own beginning and how much closer I am to my ending than my son is to his. I imagined time as a river that we all leap into at the moment of our birth, and swim down in various constellations with our family and friends until, one by one, we wash up alone along its shores. The day my son was born, I loved standing in the river and catching him in my arms, but I also dreaded that terrible, inevitable day downriver when we would be separated.

Everywhere I looked that summer, babies were dying in hot cars. I couldn't stomach any news about lost, abused, or murdered children. The rage and despair that would follow was too much. What if those things happened to my child? I would die. I was certain. I couldn't bear life without him—this tiny person I'd known only a few weeks but loved so fiercely. Nor could I bear life with him significantly harmed from something I should have been able to prevent, even if preventing it was impossible.

So I checked and rechecked his car seat every time I parked the car, especially when I didn't have him with me—because what if he was with me and I had forgotten? Any time he slept elsewhere than on my body, I stopped and laser-focused on his chest from across the room to make sure I could see its gentle, reassuring rise and fall. I tested his bath water higher and higher on my arms just in case my hands were no longer reliable temperature gauges. I eyed my partner suspiciously whenever I had to leave the two of them alone—because what if my partner had a secret violent side, or just wasn't careful enough? What if this person I chose to be my child's other parent harmed our son, intentionally or not? I would die. I would die. I would *die*.

When I imagined motherhood before I had children, I thought of sniffing fuzzy baby heads, holding tiny hands, hearing the sweet *slapslapslap* of toddler feet on the floor, cheering at soccer games, and maybe even wringing my hands over high school social drama. What I didn't, and couldn't imagine was the endless pressure, the constant feeling that I should be in control of all aspects of my child's development, that he was crying or not sleeping or not eating the right foods because I was failing at my job. Magazines and books and other parents did not help. Depending on who I consulted, I either needed to let him cry or not let him cry; I was either giving my child a sleep disorder or nurturing his attachment at any hour; I was understanding that kids' eating habits naturally evolve over time or not giving him his best nutritional start. The only unequivocal message was that parenthood wouldn't be so stressful if I could only get it right. But what exactly constituted "right" was often a matter of vicious debate.

This, combined with my anxiety and the usual social isolation of new American parenthood, put me into a dire state, one that I felt I couldn't share with others, lest I be judged—or worse, labeled a bad mother. I especially couldn't bear to risk revealing weakness to people who thought that, as one half of a same-sex couple, I should never have had a child in the first place.

One afternoon, when my son was about three months old, I called my mother, sobbing. I tried to explain how broken down I felt from my perpetual state of vigilance. She struggled to make sense of what I was saying. Her voice rose as she asked, "Are you saying you're going to hurt your baby?" "No!" I shrieked. "That's the problem! I don't want him to be hurt by anyone ever, and I can't stand the fact that he's going to be hurt somehow, somewhere, probably again and again, and there's nothing I can do about it!" *Sob. Sob. Sob.*

It's clear now, years downriver, that I was probably suffering from postpartum anxiety disorder, the manic cousin of postpartum depression. As my son got a little older and less fragile, and the wave of hormones within me crested and fell, and I got more sleep and experience, my white-knuckle grip on him eased. I started trusting my partner more. But I still thought endlessly about death, especially my own. Night was the worst. There was a black chasm in my brain, where my existential anxiety lived and multiplied. It yawned wider the longer I ignored it, until there was nowhere to look but straight into its darkness. Suddenly, I'd find myself bewildered by the universe's enormity and my own infinitesimal existence, and dumbfounded by the knowledge that millions upon millions of people have come before me and millions more will come after. From there, I wondered why I was here at all, and then on to how easily I might never have existed, and how quickly—at any moment—my existence could cease. My stomach roiled and my chest tightened as these thoughts thundered around in my head.

By day, I'd drive around the streets of my city and watch groups of addicts, young and old, dirty and bruised, morph down into babies in my mind, toddling around together on the sidewalks. I knew that many events, forces and circumstances had landed these people— these former babies—on the edge of death. Still, I wanted to know if they'd been cuddled as infants, if anyone had answered them when they cried, worried over their milestones, or sung them to sleep. I wanted them to have been loved, and found it painful to consider that they might not have been. But I also wanted to believe that if only they had good, attentive, informed mothers, they would be somewhere else, healthier and safer.

Meanwhile, it occurred to me that the sooner I had another child, the longer we'd be together in the river of time. Using a less-insane-sounding argument than that, I convinced my partner to embark on creating a sibling for our son when he was only fourteen months old. The first time around, getting me pregnant had taken six inseminations, numerous fertility treatments, and lots of money. You can imagine our shock when we succeeded on the first try. But we were happy, and while a life brewed again inside me, I was mostly able to forget about death.

Forty weeks later, on an early spring night, I pulled my second son into the river myself, surrounded by my partner, our midwife, doula, and nurse. The dim hospital room seemed to spin slowly—with our wet, pink baby at the center—as if time briefly paused its steady flow to whirl around us.

The next morning when I called our two-year-old on the phone, he burst into tears at the sound of my voice. He was sick and couldn't visit us. Not being able to comfort him nauseated me, but exposing my newborn to strep throat was not an option. My maternal circuits shorted and I melted. This was my first lesson in having to choose which child to protect more, and it stung.

The next few months were full of moments like this. When both children were crying, which was often, I had to decide who needed tending first while the waiting child's wails flooded the house and my heart banged in my chest. Some days I felt like I barely survived, but the saving grace was that I had no energy left to worry about death.

A year passed. I began a blog as a gift to myself. I found an early-morning editing job I could do from home while my family ate breakfast.

I was beginning to feel really alive again as my sons became more independent and I found more time to pursue long-shelved projects.

And then, just after our kids turned one and three, I found several enlarged lymph nodes in my groin and no infection to blame. I careened from doctor's office to doctor's office, imagining the worst. Every morning I woke up to a few seconds of peace before I remembered that I might be actively dying. Cold fear sliced through me, from my neck to my toes. My heart hammered, my throat closed. I checked my lymph nodes several times an hour to see if they'd changed. I Googled, and I Googled, and I Googled. When I couldn't Google anymore, I imagined my partner and kids floating down the river without me. I thought about what I would say in a goodbye video, or whether I should write letters to my boys instead.

These feelings and thoughts didn't come and go. They were constant, starting in the morning and not relenting until I was asleep again. Tasks that had been tedious before now seemed overwhelming. While my anxiety level remained at a debilitating high, I also experienced panic attacks that rendered me totally nonfunctional. I did my editing work, and afterward, all I could often do was curl up on the couch and cry. It was my partner's turn to worry about leaving me alone with the children.

The worst, almost unthinkable thought that tortured me was this: *I will die before my boys are old enough to remember anything about me, but especially how deeply I love them.*

This happens. Mothers of young children die all the time. I know because I read their stories online while I obsessively Googled my symptoms. In addition to the enlarged lymph nodes in my groin, I had a few in my neck, too, plus unexplained abdominal pain, and neck, jaw, and ear pain. I was certain I had lymphoma. My mother, a former nurse, kept telling me that I did not. But I thought, of course she can't fathom that I might be terminally ill. What mother wants to think about her child washed up on the river bank, while time's current drags her away?

When I went for my CT scan, I sat in the waiting area, trying not to look at the others who were waiting with me who were visibly sick. I did not want to belong there. When I was called back, I sat waiting again in a dressing room, shivering in my hospital gown, willing back tears. I exhaled loudly without realizing it, until I heard a voice say, "Is this your first time?" I peeked out the door and saw a woman poking her head out from behind a curtain. I could tell that she was bald under her scarf. I said yes, and she told me not to worry, that it wasn't so bad. Then she smiled at me. That's when my tear dam broke. I thanked her but felt a rush of fear seeing how ravaged she was followed by a shower of shame that this woman, who was obviously battling advanced disease, had the strength and energy to comfort *me*—a woman who might not be battling anything but her own demons.

Indeed, after numerous blood tests, an abdominal CT scan, a colonoscopy, ultrasounds, and a head and neck MRI, my doctors concluded that I was not dying. I did, however, have a stage zero melanoma on my upper back that was cured by excision. I had had a clean skin check only three months before, and wouldn't have had another check for nine months. It's possible then that my baffling, abrupt descent into manic anxiety—which drove me to scour my body for disease symptoms—actually did save my life. But even after that cancer was found and removed, I felt minimal relief.

During one of my last appointments, I asked my doctor why my lymph nodes were suddenly so reactive when they hadn't been before. I expected him to list possible reasons or to explain the lymph system, which I already thoroughly understood. Instead, he said, "That may just be one of life's many unanswerable questions. The older I get, the more comfortable I am with them."

In that exam room, under that fluorescent glare, surrounded by bizarre, medieval-looking ENT machinery, what this wise, grandfatherly man said was a revelation. My response to unanswerable questions—whether of the health, parenting, or existential variety—

had always been to just keep Googling. Getting "comfortable" with the unknown never occurred to me.

I decided to try it, mostly because I didn't have any other options. I had been to every doctor I could think of and had every test they could order. I had to accept at some point that what they were telling me—which was that I was making myself sick with stress and anxiety—might make more sense than my fear that I had an elusive disease that a whole lot of modern technology had so far failed to pick up on. By continuing to panic about my health problems and the possibility that they could take me away from my children, I was taking myself away from my children, and also perpetuating my health problems.

At times, paradoxically, my fear-riddled brain even suggested death as the only way out of my anxiety spiral. I will die for good one day, yes, but do I want to spend the next year—or forty years—fretting, sweating, Googling, and enacting it before it happens? Or do I want to be here now, feeling my boys' cool, soft cheeks under my lips, really getting down with them during our family dance breaks, and soaking in whatever other incredible moments I have left with them and my partner and my other loves? The answer to that question is easy. Realizing that I had a choice was the nearly impossible part.

In the middle of my summer of panic, we moved to a neighborhood with winding streets, big yards, and woods on several sides. Our cat went missing not long after. We asked neighbors if they had seen him and discovered that there were coyotes in the area. As weeks passed without our loyal Lenny coming home, we knew that he was probably dead. Our older son asked about him a lot. We told him that we thought he had died. "Why?" he asked, again and again. I tried a variety of explanations. The more I said, the more he asked why. When he asked why anyone had to die, I thought, *I am the worst person for you to ask about this*. Instead I said, "Well, buddy, I don't really know." Somehow, this answer, which made me feel like I was completely failing at an important parental task, made the most sense of all to him.

A year has passed since my medical meltdown began. Time's river seems to flow faster and faster ever forward. I still struggle with anxiety, but most days I'm able to make the conscious choice to not panic about what's around the bend, and to take my eyes off of the shores and what, if anything, lies beyond them. Instead, now I direct my nervous energy into becoming the person I want to be—for myself and for the people who are sharing this grand river-ride with me.

THROUGH DISTORTION /
ARWYN DAEMYIR

h APPY BIRTHDAY TO YOU, *happy birthday to you . . .*
I don't hear the words, just a seven-note MIDI, over and over
and over. It's preprogrammed on an electronics kit my sister-
in-law sent for Christmas, and my five-year-old has figured
out how to get it to play on continuous loop. We have a small house, and
the playroom is right in the middle: I cannot escape it. I can just hear
its tinny drone in the living room, the kitchen, the bedroom. My eye
started twitching an hour ago; my hands are tense, turning to fists in
my mind, and I force them flat in reality. *There's not a jury in the country
that would convict me!* Like all not-quite-jokes, this one sits brittle in my
head; the laughter in my mind is as sharp and off-key as the—let's be
charitable—"tune" my child happens to be obsessed with today.

I let my shoulders pull all the way up to my ears, *tight, tight, tighter,*
then exhale and release . . .

. . .

The birthday song has never been kind to us. Unlike at my child's first four birthdays, he allowed us to sing it to him this year, five candles flickering in our tiny dining room, his dad's voice and mine warbling through the all-too-familiar song. Half a dozen times that day I'd had to explain to outsiders, *No, please stop, I know it's kindly meant, but really, I need you to stop: he's only going to listen to it once, and you're not the one who gets to sing it.* Sorry, Grandma, teacher, waiter, friends.

But it's better this year than before, better to have him clamp his hands over his ears as he waits semi-patiently through unexpected renditions than his screams of terror at one year old, his screams of anger at two and three, celebrating only in secret at four to avoid any risk of someone starting to sing. He's never been a fan—of the song *or* the singing—until now.

Some people think our ban on electronic gizmos and noisemakers is a "crunchy" choice, a holier-than-thou allegiance to Waldorf or Montessori or some other exclusive philosophy. Sure, we get the Nova Naturals catalog, I know what anthroposophy is, and I can drool over math manipulatives with the best of them: It's an easy enough mistake to make. But the truth is much simpler, much less smug, and just a bit uglier. The truth is, it's quite clear where my child's aversion to crowds of people singing at him comes from, if I am at all willing to look in the metaphorical mirror.

Before having kids, I never thought of myself as having noise issues. The electronics ban, instituted before the first baby showers could bring the plastic and solder and silicon into our house, came from a lifetime of living with migraines, knowing that the last things I needed were flashing lights, electronic beeps and sirens, and an endless loop of tinny, tuneless "songs." Sensory stuff was my dad's thing, with his (then-undiagnosed) Asperger's; I may have inherited his mood swings, and okay, some of his volatility, but I wasn't like *that*. I didn't plug my ears in theaters and brag that my favorite TV channel was "off" and hit the mute switch first on every remote and gadget in my environment, and if I couldn't focus at my friend's house when the TV and the radio were both on *and* her mom was on the phone, well, that was only because I was accustomed to my dad's silent domain. Right?

Or maybe not. Maybe it took over a quarter of a century living in this noise-filled world, took parenting a child who needed airplane headphones to cut down the noise in everyday situations, and took rather more therapy than I'd care to admit, to figure out just how much auditory overwhelm runs in my family. Because I am a miserable and miserably bad parent when there's too much of the wrong kind of noise. Yelling and screeching, doors slamming, feet stomping.

That's me, not the kid.

The kid sometimes too. No, Teacher, I have no idea why he might think it's okay to slam the school door when he's having a difficult day. Sorry, we'll talk with him about it. Of course.

Like electricity, noise unbound—or wielded without care for my idiosyncrasies—is what sears; channeled and harnessed and directed by me it can soothe, give me power and strength and control. A memory: at my desk, twenty-nine other college-aspiring students around me, all bent over a particularly bothersome semi-final. I had a chain dog leash with me and kept dropping it into my hand, over and over, to hear the way it *ting*'ed together, a lovely cascade that anchored me, soothed my body so my mind could work. I didn't even realize I was doing it until one of the kids next to me hissed "Arwyn! Quit it!" and I startled out of volumes and limits and into covert glares and annoyed huffs, and put it away, cheeks burning, mind unmoored.

Now my child is the one holding the leash, experimenting with electricity, and it undoes me. I can't always know when it's going to become too much, and usually can't recognize when it has reached that threshold until after the fact, after the explosion, the yelling, the slamming, the snapping and "no!"ing and sarcasm flung at my child like stones. It starts in my neck, my body straining to retreat inside a shell it's never had. My shoulders creep up, my back rounds, my vision narrows, and my breath races high in my chest—no longer its usually slow, deep wave, but a shallow, strained pulling, *out, out, get me out, make it stop!*

Sometimes, unrecognizing, unthinking, I try to make it stop, make him stop, make the world stop, shout *stop!* Sometimes I am a shitty parent. Shit happens.

But sometimes—ah, sometimes, *I* stop. *Mama mama mama!* And I breathe. *That's not fair, I hate you, I'll never brush my teeth again!* And I bring my attention to how my breath feels trapped, my chest tight. *Waaaaaaaaaaaaaaaaaaah!* I feel the strain from pulling away, pulling back and out and down—anywhere-but-here. *Clomp, stamp, bounce, kick kick kick kick kick kick kick kick.* And I say, I need a break. Or I say, Hey, did you hear that? Or I say, I heard you say you wanted that. Or I say nothing, and be here instead, be still, be with him, be eyes that see him and arms that are hugs *in potentia,* and a body that knows—that *knows*—exactly what it is to feel overwhelmed and out of control and stuck in a world too loud, too big, too fast, too much, to be seeking for control, for power of one's own, and then, oh, then my heart breaks—breaks open, breaks boundaries, breaks free—and I am exactly, exactly the parent he needs me to be.

Happy birthday to you. . .

I go into the playroom. He's on his bed, snapping still more extraneous connections on to the already overcompleted circuit.

"Heya kiddo." *Would you mind if I smashed that to tiny plastic pieces?* No. I breathe.

"I hear you managed to get it to play without the voice activator. How'd you do that?"

I clear a space and sit down next to him, his excited explanatory babble washing through me, washing me out. The music stops and starts again as together we discover exactly which parts of the circuit are superfluous, which necessary.

This connection is necessary: his and mine, me to him, us to now. This connection doesn't cut the noise, but cuts through it, making a path for me to come inside with him, where it is sound, not noise; power, not lightning. He learns from what I do, learns not just the stomping off and slamming doors—and far too many obscenities—but also this, centering and listening and being here *now*. I cannot say which is more important, that it serves me or that through me it serves him; we two, and our best goods, are inseparable, indissoluble, and in this moment, serenaded by a stupid seven-note song, this truth has never been clearer. I am calm, and so he calms; he calms, and so I do, too.

We live surrounded by crackling static, he and I, too much noise and too many voices and tunes that turn to pain, and I am proof, like my father before me, that though he may abandon the so-stylish headphones, he may never outgrow their need. But I will sit with him, in the loudness of his world, and we will explore its edges together.

DOWN THE RABBIT HOLE /
ANNE-MARIE LINDSEY

d R. PENNY SAW THE PAIN ON MY FACE. She promised me that she would have cautioned us against pregnancy if the risks were truly unsafe. Then, this lovely woman who had witnessed so much of my journey made an even bigger promise: "I have gotten to know you, Anne-Marie. You are a wonderful person. You are going to be a wonderful mother." I held my husband, Nathan's, hand while we listened to the psychiatrist outline the risks we would face if we chose to have a baby together. The psychiatrist emphasized that no pregnancy was risk-free for any family, but that my Generalized Anxiety Disorder, Panic Disorder and Major Depressive Disorder piled on some extra risks, during and after pregnancy. Of course, there was some more risk piled on top of *that*.

I had fought hard for the "natural," medication-free pregnancy I so desperately wanted, even after I learned that many women in my position safely deliver healthy babies after being on meds during their entire pregnancies. But I lost that fight. I had spent that year, 2011, trying to wean off of my medications, Effexor and Klonopin, and then trying to switch to lower-risk medications. I had told myself that with enough preparation, my anxiety disorders and depression would disappear just in time for pregnancy and motherhood. I had gotten expert opinions, had tried no meds and then different meds; I'd even tried holistic treatments, alternative medicine, and huge shifts in my diet. Yes, all this planning had helped to alleviate my fears, but my guilt and sense of failure remained.

I had wanted to make the last effort work so badly that I had lied to Nathan and my doctor. "Yes, Ativan is working out!" I told them. Then I began having panic attacks about going to work. I stopped showing up and lost my job as an assistant teacher at a childcare center. That episode had done a lot of damage to my self-esteem and had planted more than a few doubts about my ability to "show up" as a mother. Here I was, without a job, back on the medication I had been taking when I had started seeing Dr. Penny. It was cold comfort knowing that I had done my best to achieve "minimal risk" and arrived at Decision Time.

If I succeeded in having a healthy baby after taking meds while pregnant, I would still have to choose between giving my baby breast milk that would contain traces of the medications I needed to function, versus formula, which would lack the benefits of breast milk. In both cases—in utero and out—none of the doctors who supported me could promise that any of my options would leave my child's body and brain undamaged. Even if everything seemed perfect for years after my child's birth, no one could promise me that any of my choices would ensure that child's health. I couldn't even promise that I would be all right; if I had a baby, I would face a much higher-than-average risk of postpartum mood and anxiety disorders.

I squeezed Nathan's warm hand tighter when the doctor said, "I can give you statistics and tell you that the odds are low, but you need to go and talk: What if you are the family facing the worst-case scenario?"

I wanted to be pregnant, even if I needed medication to win the battles I would face as a human being, a wife, a mother. I felt selfish for wanting to carry a child, knowing that I had lost so many battles against the chemical imbalance in my brain. But I wanted a baby with my entire being; I thought the guilt would swallow me up. Sitting in her office, I began to sob—both with pain and relief—while Nathan rubbed my back. I dabbed at my face with tissues, and we got up. I took a deep breath of crisp, fall air as we left the New York City office and headed to lunch, to have The Conversation.

There we sat in Alice's Tea Cup café, surrounded by murals depicting Alice and the strange creatures of Wonderland, staring down our own rabbit hole of percentages, inadequate studies, and uncertainties. Visiting this place I loved had been part of our plan for the day. What could be more comforting after a psychiatry and baby-planning session than tea and scones in such a magical place? I didn't think about the children who would be all around us. I watched a little girl carefully pick out fairy wings from a display inside the bakery's gift shop. Soon, we sat at a table set with mismatched tea cups, waiting for our pot of tea to arrive. It was also time to take my pills. I dug them out of my purse, and the sight of those orange bottles nearly broke me. They meant losing battles on two fronts: one, that I had failed at managing my anxiety and depression without pharmaceutical help; and second, if I became pregnant, I would be choosing the risks posed by medication over the very real and dangerous effects of panic, anxiety, and depression.

We talked. While Nathan enumerated my successes, I countered with my failings. I pointed out that I needed to take medicine every day in order to just hold down a job or remember to eat three square meals. He reminded me that going to therapy, finding the right medication, taking it every day, and treating my illness were the acts of a strong, responsible woman. Trying out new medications, trying to go off my meds, having this conversation, all before we were even trying to conceive a baby were responsible decisions. Any child we raised would see me modeling how to overcome the obstacles put in my path by genes, environment, and circumstances. It wasn't the first time he had reminded me that we were visiting New York, driving to the big city from our home in Connecticut, because we *both* knew that we would make good parents. He was right.

A good mother takes care of herself. She doesn't put herself (or her family) through daily panic attacks for the sake of a "natural" pregnancy. A good mother knows that there are risks in every choice, and that she can never protect her child from every possible danger. I fought hard to rid my body of potentially dangerous chemicals; but I also understood that the poisoned thoughts my unmedicated brain releases make taking the drugs worth the risk. No one, not even me, can say that I didn't try hard enough or that I don't deserve to bear children. Nathan was always confident about that. The day I held his hand in the doctor's office and in the cafe, I found that confidence, too.

But even if we were willing to go forward, given my diagnoses and treatment, were we prepared for the worst that might happen? When it comes to medication and pregnancy, doctors can only talk about odds and best guesses. When a company runs an ad on television that lists the potential risks and side effects of a medication, they use a list compiled by researchers who have conducted a scientific study. Those studies aren't done on pregnant women. The ethics of studying the effects of medication on the baby carried by and born to mothers taking medication are just too complicated. Dr. Penny had given us a summary of the studies that were available on Effexor during pregnancy and on Klonopin during pregnancy. The combination? We could only make an educated guess. There seemed to be a slightly increased risk of miscarriage in the first trimester. A slightly increased risk of a cleft lip and/or palate birth defect. There was a definite risk that, after the umbilical cord that separated our blood streams was cut, the baby would feel symptoms of withdrawal from my medication, including irritability, seizures, sleep problems, slow weight gain, tremors, fever, and more. The likelihood that our baby would experience full-blown symptoms like that of a baby born addicted to heroin or cocaine were very slim. But there was also the chance that my baby would experience none of it. The most likely scenario involved milder, temporary symptoms.

I already knew that I would give up the home birth I had always wanted; I would give birth in a hospital, even though hospitals terrified me, so that experts would be on hand to deal with any birth defects or withdrawal symptoms. In other words, instead of a peaceful arrival into our family and our home, my baby's first days outside my body could be filled with pain, and we might need specialists to help mitigate that pain. Nathan and I agreed to take that risk because I would give birth in one of the best children's hospitals in the world, just a five minute drive from home. If the baby was born with a cleft lip, a cleft palate, and withdrawal symptoms, we would grieve. Talented doctors would step in immediately, however, and make sure that he or she made a full recovery with no more than a scar to show for it and certainly no memories of any pain. We hated the idea, of course. Was it enough to stop us from taking the chance and having a baby? No. Was the risk of miscarriage enough to stop us? No.

The incredible lesson we learned that day was that no one would ever be able to point to anything during a pregnancy, birth, or new life and say "*that* happened because Anne-Marie took Effexor and Klonopin." All of it—even the symptoms associated with withdrawal— can happen to anyone, even a mother with a clean bill of health and no illness or medication before or during her pregnancy. In my quest for perfection, I had never stopped to consider that healthy families experience loss and illness with no explanation. It had never occurred to me that deciding to expand a family could set any couple down a path to pain and suffering. If the Good Mother in my imagination couldn't even promise her family a perfect baby, maybe it was time to reevaluate what being a good mother would mean to *my* family.

Nathan and I left New York City that day confident in our decision to try to conceive a child. We headed back home confident in the knowledge that we would be good parents, and that our family would remain strong, no matter the outcome.

Just a few months later, in early 2012, I became pregnant. My pregnancy was blessedly free from complications. The ultrasounds pointed to a healthy, active fetus. We made it through. And before long, we saw a healthy, active baby boy.

His birth was the single most empowering event in my life. I felt calm and strong, and I had so much faith in my body and my baby. He was born in perfect health. He didn't cry, but he was a healthy pink. His eyes opened. He gripped our fingers. His muscle tone was a bit higher than normal, and while he was too sleepy to nurse at first, there were no signs of withdrawal or pain. I asked if my medications were causing any problems. The doctors and nurses said that he wasn't in any pain, and that we could feed him from a syringe. In fact, he roused so quickly, my midwife nicknamed him "the little monkey" because he never seemed to stop moving. And Klonopin is supposed to be a sedative . . .

To this day, our son, Walter James Lindsey, has never experienced a single health problem. And though my anxiety and depression have not disappeared, I am managing them.

The happy family I fought so hard to have is *here*.

FAILURE TO LAUNCH /
KIMBERLY MORAND

BRIGHT MORNING SUNRAYS DANCED across our city's skyline and forced their way through the tiny windows of room 380. "Focus, Kim," said the gentle masked voice hidden beyond my swollen belly. "Just one more time."

I drew in a large breath and held on to it tighter than my anxious husband was gripping my hand. I put everything I had into that one final push. At 6:56 AM on August 14, 2008, our son was born.

"I'm so glad that I was still here to be a part of this," my night nurse said as she laid the tiny swaddled soul on my chest. I lightly grazed my finger across his reddened cheek and drew back his oversized knit cap. His hair was thick and black, blacker than any night sky that I had ever wished upon for this exact miracle to happen.

I sunk deeply into the hospital bed. I could feel him whispering soft breaths on the nape of my neck. His body curled perfectly into mine, as if my body was born molded for this moment. Then I waited for my heart to swell with love, just like every mom had told me it would, but I felt nothing. Emptiness washed over me. My soul dropped to the bottoms of my feet, and I pounded my head back against the pillow.

I knew immediately that something was wrong.

I had just made a terrible mistake.

Over the next few days, my life was nothing short of chaotic. No person or book can ever prepare you for the torture that is called colic. The witching hour, as we dubbed it, started every night at seven o'clock. He would scream incessantly for hours. Those shrill wails, punctuated by the false promise of brief silences when it seemed his little body had no energy left to force out another sound, had worn my patience right down to the bone. Hours seemed to run into days and then into weeks as my sleep dwindled down to thirty-minute pockets here and there in a twenty-four hour period.

My nerves were frayed raw, and I found myself lost in rapidly changing waves of anxiety and anger. I was given to violent outbursts: I put holes in our walls, my foot through a wicker chair, I smashed glass, and gouged my own skin with deep scratches. I had absolutely no control. I had a solid support system at my disposal, but I didn't reach out for help. I was terrified of what everyone would think of me; perhaps label me crazy and try to take my baby away.

I worked hard to keep my failing sanity a secret by creating a happy façade in our home. I greeted visitors with fake smiles to veil the demons that lurked inside my head. I awkwardly went through the motions of what I thought a "good, loving" mother would do. The harder I fought to ignore my emotional pain, the harder it fought to have its ever-looming existence acknowledged. The visitors hugged me tightly and kissed my son's cheek goodbye. I was sad when they left me because I didn't want to be left alone with him.

I remember one day, after my guests had left, I carried my son down to his nursery. The window was open and warm winds flowed in, laced with the scent of fresh grass clippings. I relaxed into the antique rocking chair with him, relishing the feel of the sun's rays cascading down on us.

I stared into his dark eyes as we rocked, trying, wishing, and praying that I would feel love for him as effortlessly as my friends and family did. The weight of his body felt as heavy as the overwhelming emotions that suffocated me daily.

As I held my son, he began to squawk like he always did around that time, and the high-pitched noise curdled my blood. I had already fed him, changed him, and pretended to love him. "What else do you need?!" I shouted over his screams.

I started rocking faster and faster as my mind wandered. I fantasized about what it would be like to place this screaming bundle on the floor and run out of there. I'd tear through the grass in my bare feet and climb my neighbor's fence. I didn't know where I would go, but I clung to the simple thought of leaving him and my newly defined role as a terrible mother far behind. Imagining being normal again gave me a thrilling release from the relentlessness of my pressurized existence.

I looked down, feeling a wave of guilt, and saw that his face had reddened and strained through his fits. I felt suddenly sure that if I didn't distance myself from him, right then and there, I would lose it. With great care, I placed him back in his crib as he continued to bawl and walked into the bathroom, locking the door behind me. I slid down the wall and leaned my elbows deep into my thighs. I took my index fingers and dug them into both ears to drown out all the noise. Then I closed my eyes and wished that he would just disappear.

As each day passed, my symptoms worsened. Thoughts ran faster than I could process. It felt like 500 television channels were all on at once and I couldn't turn them off. It made decision-making absolutely impossible. I remember standing in front of my closet for hours panicking about what outfit I should wear for the day. The anxiety became so bad that I was terrified to leave my own home. I soon started to isolate myself from the outside world.

In order to gain some control, I started cleaning the house at ungodly hours and obsessing over unnecessary lists about feeding, changing, and sleeping times. Things had to be done correctly all the time. For instance, my son's washcloths had to be folded four times and placed on color-coordinated stacks. I would do it over and over again until it was perfect, and even then it still wasn't good enough.

Throughout this entire time, my husband insisted that I wasn't well. I would lash back at him, saying that I was perfectly fine and that I didn't have postpartum depression. I did not fall in the very minimal "cookie cutter" list of symptoms that was provided in a pamphlet from the hospital. On the cover was a woman who was disheveled and exhausted, holding a crying infant. I was not "that" mom, because I wasn't depressed at all.

When I was five weeks postpartum, my husband and I stood in a friend's wedding. Eager first-time grandparents offered to babysit our son and even told us to take the night "off." I welcomed the break without hesitation. I watched as my dad slowly and carefully picked my son up from the car seat. He cradled him close to his heart and said, "You're going to miss him, aren't you?"

My chest tightened as anger boiled inside my stomach. I wanted to scream. I hated that my son cried. I hated that I couldn't sleep even when I had help. I hated that I was terrified of leaving my house. I hated that my mind wouldn't shut off. I hated that I couldn't handle the demands of motherhood. In fact, I hated being a mother, period.

I hated that I didn't love my son like everyone else did.

I woke up the next morning to my husband's soft whisper, "We have to go." I peered at the clock and started to cry. I didn't want to go get him.

We drove to my parents' house with the windows wide open. I tucked my legs into my chest and my dress crept up my thighs. Wind blasted through the windows and stirred my hair in every direction. Instead of hurrying to gather and save each lock, I let it go.

I wanted to feel free.

When we pulled into my parents' driveway, I reached for my husband's arm to stay in the car for just a minute longer. I took in a breath and looked at my husband through tears and asked him one question:

"Do you love him?"

"Of course I do," he replied without hesitation. "Don't you?"

I didn't answer.

My parents met us at the doorway, showering him with all the love they had. I wanted that. I knew I was going to have to fight for it.

The following week, at my six-week postpartum assessment, I sat on the high stretcher wearing only a thin plastic sheet that separated my dignity and the doctor. My husband sat anxiously in the corner as I mouthed, "There is something wrong with me."

My ob-gyn lifted his face from behind my chart as I spoke. I explained to him the overwhelming anger and anxiety that had stolen my smile, my laughter, and my strength. That it came in crushing oppressive waves that pulled me down deeper into murky waters every single day. I felt as if I was watching my world from beneath these waters. So far removed that no matter how hard I tried to swim, I couldn't break the surface.

It was inescapable and some days it was just easier to not swim at all.

"I'm a terrible mom," I shakily said, "I don't even love him."

He took a deep breath and said, "Kimberly, you're not a bad mom and you're not crazy. You have postpartum depression."

My fight to bridge the gulf back to myself—and to my son— started that very day.

Recovering from postpartum depression and anxiety was not an easy process. I was very blessed to receive quick and compassionate care from my doctors, for which I will forever be grateful, and for my support system of friends and family who surrounded me with love.

On the road to recovery, there were setbacks, but as I continued the fight, they grew fewer and farther apart. That is the key to this battle. To keep fighting. I stumbled. There were times when I reached the end of the month, week, day, or hour and I had simply nothing left for anyone or anything, not even myself. There were times when I thought the only way forward was to start back at square one. Sometimes I actually had to. Other times, I would stop and look back. Look back at how far I'd come. For each time I stumbled, I got stronger and wiser.

Tonight, four years after winning that epic battle, I find myself standing in my son's doorway after he's fallen asleep. When the furnace kicks on, and the curtains begin to flutter, casting shadows that dance across the room. I watch as his chest deeply and rhythmically rises and falls with every breath. His pudgy toes peek from under the covers. I feel such peace watching him sleep.

I always do.

I stand there quietly for a while longer, amazed at how this powerful fleeting moment can still sweep me off my feet. This little soul has made my heart swell with so much love.

I can't recall the exact moment I fell in love with him or how I fell in love with him, but it took time. Now, I can't even imagine a love greater than the love I have for my son.

He's the reason I sought help.

He's the reason I breathe.

Postpartum depression is as real as cancer, diabetes, and heart disease. It can be treated. All you need to do is reach out your hand and someone will grab it and never let it go.

We are not alone in this.

We are worth this fight.

We are beautiful.

We are loved.

In all its pain and beauty, we are mothers to the end.

THE PECULIAR CURSE OF MENTALLY ILL MOTHERHOOD /
SHANNON DRURY

Since my early teens I have suffered from chronic anxiety and severe depression, but only since my first child was born was I sufficiently motivated to seek appropriate treatment, as my usual coping mechanisms of alcohol, sorrowful alt-country albums, and furiously self-indulgent journaling were no longer available to me. Motherhood made me finally acknowledge these serious threats to my health, which is why I rarely, if ever, think of myself as a *person* with mental illness. I am something far more dangerous and frightening—I am a mentally ill *mother*.

This is a terrible thing to admit, let alone understand. Even now, I equivocate: I write in a passive voice, I bury the information at the end of my sentences, I crack stale Prozac jokes, I let acquaintances think I am running off to Meetings of Professional Importance that are in fact intensive hours of therapy.

In contrast, I hardly mourned when my son was diagnosed with Asperger's Syndrome when he was seven. After all, as countless psychologists reminded me, this was likely the same neurological quirk that made Bill Gates the wealthiest man in the world. Hell, in my wholly overeducated social circle (I am one of very few with "just" a bachelor's degree), you'd be hard pressed to find a young boy *without* a spot on the autism spectrum. Even the discussion of emotional anguish in our children occurs without much eyelash-batting, for only a *truly engaged* mother cares enough about junior's nail-biting to wonder if it might be evidence of a condition requiring professional intervention. You're going to fix it. You are a good mother.

I doubt such compassion exists for nail-biting moms, or to be more accurate, cuticle-ripping, nail bed-slashing moms, the ones dripping so much blood they must stanch the flow with the hems of their black t-shirts. I do this when I am uncomfortable, which is nearly all the time. Do other parents notice this? Was my terror conspicuous today, when I brought my children to the start of a fresh week of summer classes at the local high school? Did the teenage instructors see my right thumb, mummified on the edge of my shirt?

The peculiar curse of an anxiety disorder is the terrible warping of reality that occurs when an episode is at its peak. Camp counselors cannot be bothered to monitor the hands of their charges' mothers, of course, but this is not obvious until much later, long after *Toy Story* Band-Aids have been applied to each offending finger. The knowledge that could save me, that *no one else cares* as much as I seem to, is cruelly withheld until it is no longer of any therapeutic use.

My own mother is also mentally ill, but she is not my ally. She cannot offer me support, nor will she, for the peculiar curse of her own condition requires that she strenuously object to any characterization of herself as a less than ideal parent. A few times a year, we sit before a beleaguered family therapist, on the pretense of repairing our perhaps fatally fractured relationship. My mother complains that I am too sensitive, then argues that my childhood memories are either distorted or false.

"Mom, you have bipolar disorder," I sigh. My mother nods. "And you weren't treated for it until I left for college," I add. She nods again, and I ask the question that I never intended to be rhetorical: "How could that *not* affect me?"

"But you never wanted for anything," she tells me. This six-word phrase, repeated so many times that it could be a psychotherapeutic drinking game (but not for Mom, an alcoholic, *quelle surprise*), is the mantra she repeats to keep the worst of her demons at bay. If she looked deeply into the truth of her illness, saw it reflected in the eyes of her terrified young daughter, her suffering would be unendurable. She needs me to stop asking her to do this. "You just want me to admit that I'm a bad mother, is that it?" she says.

For a moment I regret leaving my Aspie son at home. Elliott, now a preteen and an expert snarler, moaner, and mutterer-under-the-breath, could easily deflate her with a snarktastic "OH SURE, LIKE THAT WOULD JUST FIX EVERYTHING." At forty, I tell myself I'm not that stupid, but in reality, I'm not that brave.

Elliott, it should be noted, sees a cognitive behavioral therapist who gave him a copy of *What to Do When You Grumble Too Much: A Kid's Guide to Overcoming Negativity*, a workbook with an entire chapter devoted to drawings of cups filled to their precise midpoint, which the book's target audience would describe as half-empty. In Elliott's case, he might check to see how much his sister's cup held before he formed an opinion, and even then he might argue the relative merits of a half-cup of water versus lemonade, Pepsi, chocolate sauce, red wine, or Clamato. To an Aspie, not even a psychological exercise can be taken at face value.

I wish I had *his* diagnosis, not mine.

Am I a bad mother? I ask myself. I ask my therapist, my husband, the few friends who know of my Prozac, Neurontin, and Ativan regimen.

Their answer is invariably no, but what else could it be? Who would tell me if I were?

My seven-year-old daughter, Miriam, bites her nails. She chews them down to angry red nubs that even I, her loving (good!) mother, must admit are really quite ugly. "It's a bad habit," she laments, using language she learned from a Berenstain Bears book on the subject. "I want to stop it, but I can't." I tell her I know how she feels. When I was her age, my fingers were raw and bloody too, like the tips of ten half-eaten hot dogs. I made countless attempts at quitting, abandoning the habit completely when an anxiety-triggered jaw clenching disorder made gnawing on anything small and tough impossible (another curse of mental illness is that it rarely manifests itself in the head alone). I spare her this long story, opting instead to merely offer evidence of my own fingers, brutalized in a slightly different fashion. "OWIE," she says, shocked. Could she have believed that my Band-Aids were an expression of fashion? She knew that what little jewelry I wore was for meaning, not ornamentation: a wedding band on my left hand, an anniversary band on my right. I wasn't a fancy person. I wouldn't wear Band-Aids for fun, would I?

Little girls don't know why their mothers do anything. A mother remains mysterious, wrapped in an invisible Band-Aid of maternal invincibility until such time as she is exposed, either by time, by accident, or by deliberate, compassionate confession. "If you want to stop biting your nails," I tell her, "you can try. Do your best, but don't beat yourself up about it. Try to let it go, if you can. They're only fingernails."

That I try to mother my children the way I wish my own mother had cared for me is unremarkable; most, if not all, parents wish to improve upon the mistakes of the previous generation. What *is* remarkable is that I am still not able to extend the same kindness and compassion to myself. When nervous tension builds, and it invariably does, I am more than unkind—I am merciless. My fingers bleed, but the real violence occurs internally. The deep love I hold for my children has a frightening doppelganger in the contempt I have for myself.

. . .

My mother cries in our sessions, but I rarely do. In these meetings, I am scrupulously left-brained, monitoring her outbursts for clues that could unravel the mentally ill mother's pathology; I often suspect I am taking more mental notes than the therapist herself, who seems genuinely baffled by our stubborn lack of progress. "What do you both want out of this?" she asks.

"I want to move forward," my mother wails.

"I want to understand what's happening in my head so I can be a better mother to my children," I reply, and a teary wave washes on the shore of our therapist's white leather couch. I didn't say I wanted to be a better mother than *her*, exactly, but this is what she hears. In our sessions I admitted to my mother for the first time that my anxiety is so great I resort to self-injury to cope, and that suicidal thoughts have plagued me since I was a fifth grader. Her face, though damp, remained blank; the genetic connection between our two illnesses is also a sore subject. Do family trees dealing with hereditary, but nonpsychiatric, conditions grapple with this? Do diabetic parents refuse to monitor the blood sugar of their offspring as a matter of pride? Surely a mother could hold herself blameless for the random organization of chromosomes in her child's DNA. Not so the mentally ill mother, whose protective distortions cocoon her in a reality that is unaffected by either nature *or* nurture.

Our therapist sighs. "Do you want to meet again next month?"

I save my emotions until I leave the clinic and have driven myself to the Whole Foods located half a mile away. Purged of tears and six or seven cuticles, I troll the supermarket aisles, gobbling third helpings of cheese samples and wrapping my fingers in the accompanying napkins.

My mother serves an important function in my mental health regimen, almost in spite of herself. Her purpose is not to offer solace or even guidance as I wander through the sludge of depression or the spikes of anxiety. She warns me. She is a reminder that for my children to be successful (meaning that they are emotionally functional, though I remain hopeful that an Aspie spark might finance my early retirement), I have no choice but to work harder. I have to work harder than she did, and I have to work harder than the other moms at summer camp drop-off do. I have no choice. It is my particular curse.

I wrap my hands in whatever is handy, and I carry on.

PART IV

MAMA BY ANY OTHER NAME

THE INVISIBLE MOTHER /
SHAY STEWART-BOULEY

OW COULD I HAVE KNOWN?
For a long time, I tortured myself with that question.
The day I sent my six-year-old son off to his father's for
Christmas, hundreds of miles away from me, how could I
have known I would cease to be his custodial mother? How could I have
known that the last six years of our life together, during which I'd raised
him myself while working full-time, fully invested in his little life—in
our little life—would abruptly end? And that my role as mother, in the
traditional sense, would be wrested from me against my will?

The fateful day broke cold, even by Chicago standards—maybe
that should have been a sign. I was worried about getting him on the
airplane, as this would be his first time flying as an unaccompanied
minor, so I was more impatient than normal. More anxious.

"Son, get your buns over here," I said, using a brusque voice to force down my urge to weep. He shuffled over, and I straightened what needed straightening, smoothed what needed smoothing. Rubbed his nose with mine. "Nosey, nosey, nosey," we said in our usual mantra.

My attentions were the almost unconscious, but still intense, hands-on nature of mothering that I had been doing solo for almost six years at that point. It was reflex in addition to love. When I hugged him, kissed him, and he said, "Bye, Mom," I sent him off with tears already beginning to form, already eager for his return from Christmas with his Dad.

They wouldn't be the last tears or the most fierce ones.

Because my son didn't come back.

Up until that point, my ex-husband—my son's father—had chosen to remain on the sidelines of our son's life. We'd had a brief, volatile affair, then married too young, got pregnant, and became estranged and separated well before our son had even turned two. I'd finally gotten my divorce from him when my son was five-and-a-half, freeing me up to marry the man I'd been dating since my boy was four.

However, I didn't anticipate how much it would chafe my ex-husband's ego to know another man would have a daily role in his son's life—never mind that he was a mild-tempered man with no aims to replace him as a father, only to fit in.

My ex-husband's answer to the problem was brutally efficient. Without consulting me, he decided he wanted sole custody of our son. Or, rather, he simply did not put my son on the scheduled return flight home the day it arrived.

The only thing that flew that day was my heart. Shredded and wrested from my chest, it fluttered desperately, fruitlessly, toward Maine, to my son, leaving the rest of me behind in Chicago.

All I had left were tears. Self-recrimination. And fear. *How was my son? What was his father telling him about me? When would I ever see him again?!*

As added torture, little did I know that not only was I about to become invisible to my son as a mother, but also to the rest of the world as well. The day he didn't come home, my status as a mother was unceremoniously stripped from me by the outside world.

Unless you've lost a child to someone else, you cannot know the fierce pain and desolation that comes in the aftermath. The despair, the worrying, the surreal quality that you're living another person's life and not your own. The aching sense of powerlessness you feel as a mother when your child needs you most. Did he miss me? Was he terrified? Did he cry himself to sleep, curled in despair and anxiety? Simply put, it is a tragedy beyond measure. During our phone conversations, which sometimes were separated by days no matter how hard I tried to get through, I did my best to be strong—to help him be strong—to let him know that no matter what, I was still his momma.

When he would say, "I'm okay" or "Everything's good," it was hard to tell if he was trying to make me feel better or telling the truth. But we could still connect. I could still be a mother, however awkwardly, however far removed by the miles.

A fast and furious legal battle ensued, and we ended up with joint legal custody. In a painful twist, primary residence was awarded to my ex: my son and I would now be separated by 1,100 miles, hardly a good setup for traditional "joint" custody. I didn't want to drag our son through a long countersuit or make him have to "choose" between parents, nor could I afford to. Besides, I felt certain that, based on my husband's past behavior, he would tire of being a full-time dad and send our son back to me. He was punishing me, I told myself. My son would come home.

I was wrong, and I was relegated to the status of "noncustodial" mother, a term that in our culture is a stigma, loaded with innuendo, failure, and neglect. I did not love my son any less; I did not invest any less in his life, his care, and his needs. I simply had to do it from afar and make the best of short trips to visit him. For his sake, I stayed positive and supportive and did my best to reinforce a sense of stability and security for him in this new dynamic. He flourished while I quietly suffered. Not only because I missed him, but also because, at best, to be a noncustodial mother is to be invisible to the eyes of the world around you.

We live in a society that only sees mothering through a narrow lens: If a mother is not physically with her children, we assume she is not a mother—or at least not a loving and good one. When we hear the term "noncustodial mother," we assume the worst of her. She clearly must have issues. Is she mentally unstable? An addict? Or is she simply cold, lacking any maternal instinct? Judgment is quick and harsh, a knee-jerk reaction to the antithesis of what is presumed to be a Good Mother.

Precisely because I *was* a loving mother and needed to be near my son, I would eventually be the first to wave the white flag and move across the country to be closer to him, despite the fact it would devastate both my career track and my husband's. But by the time I was able to make that happen, I had spent four years living more than a thousand miles away from my son.

During those years, I traveled as frequently as I could to see him, maxing out my credit cards with airfare, hotels, and the cost of little adventures to make the best of our once-a-month visits together. But those facts aren't evident in the brief exchange when a person learns you're a noncustodial mother. None of those people saw the countless packages of carefully selected clothes I sent to him, since I still held the responsibility of buying and replacing the ones he'd outgrown. Nor did they hear me on the phone scheduling his biannual physicals with his pediatrician, or how I managed his vaccinations and teeth cleanings, or read him stories over the phone. They didn't know that those rare times my son was being a difficult child, his father would have him call me, knowing that hearing me say, "I'm disappointed that you did that" could have more impact from half a country away than a punishment from his father would.

My son was no longer under my roof, but he was still my primary responsibility and the center of my heart. But the distance was like a cancer, and I grew to believe that somehow I was a defective woman for "allowing" my son to live with his father.

The painful part is that when I did move to be closer to him so that I could truly have joint custody, nothing much changed from society's perspective. Whether I was in Chicago or New England, I would often be subjected to the same level of scrutiny and judgment when people realized I had a child but not custody. Questions like, "Why doesn't your son live with you?" or "How did you lose custody?"—as if I'd failed my child, which meant failing as a mother.

When my ex moved to a different (but at least adjacent) state, and I started racking up thousands of miles of extra car travel so that my son could spend most weekends with me, I got adept at telling people, "My son goes to school in New Hampshire" in a tone that shut down further inquiry. If their brains jumped to the conclusion that he went to boarding school, all the better. My son picked up the same habit over the years when he spent holidays with me and my husband, saying to people, "I go to school out of state."

Sometimes, other kids would press him about why he didn't live with me. "It was like they didn't think you were involved, or didn't care, or didn't exist," he told me once. "It made me mad, Ma. Sometimes, they'd even tell me I was a liar when I said I lived for years with you in Chicago."

For me, what hurt the most personally was when someone would tell me—or make the implication when they didn't say it outright—that I didn't know what it was like to raise a child since my son no longer lived with me, as if mothering is only possible when you are physically with your child every single day. In the four years we were apart, I went back to school and earned my bachelor's degree—for that I was called selfish. Never mind that years later, when my son would apply to college, my own experiences of having been through college and graduate school would prove vital in helping him navigate the maze of applying to universities. Never mind that by going back to school myself, I could earn enough money to help put him through college.

Never mind that I set the bar high for him, and he would end up clearing it.

Instead, most people only saw a woman who "allowed" her son to live with his father. I would learn, in time, that no matter what anyone else thought or said about me, my power as a mother was still as great—and just as important to him—no matter how far the physical distance between us.

When my son was thirteen, I gave birth to my second child, a girl. While I was no longer insecure in my parenting abilities, I did notice that by virtue of the fact that my daughter was physically present with me, people's perceptions of me as a mother had changed. Suddenly I was seen as a "real" mother; I was now, by default, a part of the maternal tribe. Never mind that I had already been moving in that same circle, invisible, for thirteen years.

That's when I started to speak up.

I remember the day that my daughter started kindergarten and someone commented how hard it was to let our kids go—funny thing was that the same week my daughter started kindergarten, my son started college almost 1,300 miles away. And I pointed this out, that I was letting two kids go at the same time.

"But it's not the same, though, right?" the other mother said, once she had gotten the very short and highly sanitized version of my custodial history. "You're used to him not living with you."

"He spent the first six years of his life just with me; this isn't my first time seeing a child off to kindergarten," I said. "Just a kid with a very different personality."

"But, well . . . going off to college after all these years not living with you," the mother corrected herself, suddenly aware she'd hit a nerve but unaware she hadn't really been any less insulting by changing her approach.

"It's still a transition. It's still letting go," I answered. "This is new territory for him and for me. I've still been a big part of raising him for eighteen years."

Once again, my right to claim my status as my son's mother had been challenged by someone else because he had "already been living away from me." This time, however, I didn't play along. I was quick to point out why that theory was wrong.

I owned and declared my motherhood.

When I started my parenting journey twenty-one years ago, I was ambivalent. After all, finding yourself married and pregnant at eighteen is scary. Yet when I was that young, I never envisioned what my motherhood journey would look like. I went through the same highs and lows with my son that any mother experiences with her kids, and while they have not always happened under my roof, my son has always been in my heart and thoughts, even when he was not physically with me. I still gave him advice and comfort. I still had the phone or email.

Now, when my son comes home from college for a holiday or for the summer, he often engages me in the hour right before or after midnight for a long heart-to-heart in the kitchen, and not so long ago he said to me, "I know you still worry about the past, Ma, but I always knew I could count on you. I didn't always understand what was happening or why, but I knew I had a mom *and* a dad—and I never thought you didn't care."

I was always a part of his life. I was always his mother. Present to him even in my physical absence.

The rest of the world might have seen me as invisible in terms of motherhood, but my son did not. I still feel a sting when I think of all the lost years I didn't get to *watch* him grow up, but I am comforted that he felt me walking alongside him the entire journey.

THE ADOPTION AISLE /
SARAH WERTHAN BUTTENWIESER

SOMEONE AT THE CAFÉ ASKS me how many children I have.
"Four," I answer. "The oldest is sixteen and the youngest, my daughter, is just four."

The woman raises her eyes. I get this look often, the four-is-double-two look.

I nod. "I know. *Four*." And then I offer, "The last one we adopted. I didn't mean to have four children, but it wasn't exactly accidental."

"Oh," the woman I've never met—a friend of a friend—exclaims, just a bit too loudly. "Where is she from?" This next question is rapid fire, an autopilot follow up to the "your child is adopted" revelation.

"Worcester," I answer. No tales of China or Guatemala or Vietnam here. "I was at her birth," I offer. "It's an open adoption."

"That's so *good* of you," the woman says, as if adoptive parenthood is some sort of volunteer activity. On the list of things I never attempted to *be* by adopting a baby, good is at the top. If I were to spill the whole story then and there, with my iced tea sweating on the rickety outdoor two-top, I'd begin this way: I did not know my daughter's birth mother before her pregnancy, and as a result, much as I love her—and I do—I did not adopt a baby to help another woman out. I did so because my husband and I decided we wanted one more baby, our little girl.

The woman's friend, my friend, interjects, "She's so cute, that little girl."

I smile, as does the friend I'm sitting with, and we all agree she's adorable. When the inquisitor goes inside to grab her iced drink, my friend leans over, "Exotic Worcester," she says wryly. I am so used to this, I almost forget how many what-not-to-say things people actually say to me.

There is something deeply uncomfortable about those moments when someone praises me for adopting my own child or asks something intrusive about the adoption or misuses the word *real* to refer to biological ties. It's not that praise or questions or even vocabulary upend me; I'm pretty matter-of-fact about adoption. What I find hard is the underlying assumption in the praise or questions or language—that "adoptive" makes the mother or the father of the child *a little less than*.

Less than a straight shot from egg and sperm, to uterus to arms.

For a society that will tinker with any "natural" process—birth, death, aging, noses, or chicken pox—this clinging to the old-fashioned "man and woman make a baby" mode as the truest path to motherhood is, when you think about it, rather odd. Witnessing my daughter's birth as, essentially, a bystander, I promise I'm not less of a mother to her. I'm not like her mother; I *am* her mother.

That doesn't mean it was easy to stand in the hospital room through the early hours on a winter's morning and wait for the teeny, tiny girl to emerge from her mother's body. Her mother, Caroline, was afraid of childbirth, the physical pain compiled by the impossible task on the other side of that physical feat—to let go of her daughter's tiny fingers, the ones that would naturally grasp her finger. Short version: It was the most excruciatingly joyous moment I've ever experienced. My daughter's birth, our daughter's—ours, being Caroline's, mine, my husband Hosea's—was, as birth really always is, beautiful and filled with possibility and hope, but the loss hung in the room as well, thick enough to breathe in, loud as Caroline's sobs after Saskia arrived.

The hospital was not accommodating. Hospital policy didn't let anyone into the nursery, and though Hosea and I were promised a room beforehand, we were refused that courtesy once the day came, so the only place we could hold the baby was in Caroline's room. The upside was that we got to know Caroline's family better—which now, in its way, is our family too—and we met her friends, and her friends and family met Saskia, and we all bonded—the group of us—against the evil behemoth that was Saint Vincent's Hospital, and most especially its judgmental nursing staff.

I never expected to leave a newborn in a nursery overnight an hour from home, but that turned out to be the best thing to do for everyone involved. To stay with the baby meant that we'd be in Caroline's room with her and we understood that she needed the rest and the break. She had to find her maternal resolve to stick to her decision, one complicated by a tiny, mewing, perfect creature she couldn't ignore all day long, even if she wasn't changing her diapers, or feeding her, or holding her nonstop (though she held her as much as she asked to).

I never expected that taking the curves in the parking garage from the backseat of our station wagon beside a newborn in an infant bucket seat would feel like riding in a getaway car from a bank heist, or that this would be a sensation of parenthood, but there you go.

Once home, I switched formulas and found breast milk from women who had too much, and put my baby to my bare chest without fear a nurse would happen in while Caroline was outside having a smoke. I started to calm down a little bit. I started to feel like Saskia's mother.

Although I couldn't wholly comprehend it yet, those hospital days were being her mother, too. Motherhood could be defined like this: You discover your willingness to do for your child things you never imagined yourself capable of doing.

Nor was it easy not to be able to make the milk that would sustain her, having breastfed her three older brothers. Early on in the process, I took fifteen-minute chunks away from everyone to sit with the breast pump, hoping the sucking action would stimulate milk production. To no avail.

Day after day in those first weeks home, my husband would tape the Supplemental Nursing System (SNS) tubes to my breasts, the ends just at my nipples, a bottle of milk around my neck. The idea of the SNS is that a baby will get milk while at the breast, and that at best, this may stimulate production, too. In any case, the baby gets milk and breast together, even if not from one source.

Still, those good intentions were met with reality. She was tiny— well under six pounds—and she wasn't yet a strong sucker. Trying to get the tube into her tiny mouth along with my massive nipple was quite challenging. I couldn't manipulate the parts alone—the parts being breast, tube, and baby—with just two hands, since one was busy cradling her. Even with my husband's assistance, she really couldn't figure out how to extricate the milk from the thin tube, let alone effectively suckle at the breast. Meantime, there were three more kids in the house. Those precious fifteen-minute chunks of time at the pump, and more at the breast, took me away from them. And they needed our attention as we transitioned from a family of five to a family of six. For everyone's sake, the bottle made much more sense.

The bottle meant I wasn't the only one to feed her, the way I had done for her brothers. Instead, she was held and nurtured by her papa and each of her brothers—who at the time of her arrival were five, nine, and twelve. It took work on my part to feel okay about not being the only one to feed her. Rather than feel inadequate about what I wasn't able to provide—my breasts—instead I felt supremely grateful for what I *could* provide: a loving family with plenty of arms (mine included) that loved to hold and nurture her while she fed, which is ultimately the reason we moms breastfeed. We want to nurture our babies well beyond nutritional concerns. I had to grow my definition of mother, to push myself to cede something in order to gain more.

Meantime, I had to hold tight to that feeling—*mother*—because the whole question of telling came up almost immediately, and comes up frequently with an adopted infant. Saskia has dark hair and dark eyes, and her skin is on the pale side for a biracial child. For a white gal, I have pretty dark skin, along with dark hair that's going grey and dark eyes. My boys, by comparison, are relatively fair: one has green eyes and dark hair, the second is dirty-blonde with brown eyes, and the third boy has blond hair and blue eyes. Go figure. So this girl, she happens to resemble me. People think she does, and indeed, when I imagined her before she was born, she looked exactly like this—like me. I was rounder than her, with bigger cheeks, mistaken for Asian and Inuit and Mexican and just about everything else. No one said Jamaican of me, but that's what she is on her father's side.

Almost as soon as I started to go places—the grocery store, for example—people voiced their assumptions. I carried her in a fleece sling and so they peeked in. "When did you have her?" someone might ask.

I didn't, I wanted to say. I didn't look postpartum, and so I got stares of the how-did-she-do it variety. The answer was that I hadn't, and we were in the process of adopting her, and it was open, and I was at her birth, but how many times are you supposed to share that story—and with strangers?

And sometimes, when people said to me, "She's beautiful," I felt bad accepting the compliment. I wanted to tell Caroline about each admirer. I wanted her to experience the part of that flattery that comes when your genetic material rearranges itself with someone else's to give you a gorgeous baby. But she knew how beautiful Saskia was, and she shared pictures, and people affirmed this to her.

When I ran into someone I knew, the other person would inevitably say, "I didn't know you were pregnant." In those instances, it was easy to tell the short version of how she came into our lives. I'd skip the sadness in the labor room, the tension in the hospital, and the near-thievery in the parking garage. I'd share just the highlights as I stood in the market aisle, doing the tell-tale mama-jostle as my daughter rustled in the carrier: all unconscious knee bends and side-to-side swaying that one does as a primitive response to soothe babies.

Sometimes, though, when a stranger asks about her, I *do* tell the whole story. And if it takes place at Whole Foods, the chances are very high that the person I have told will tell me, "I'm an adoptive parent, too. Biggest gift in my whole life." I can't say why this happens so frequently at Whole Foods, but it does, and I soon became convinced that if you are considering adoption and want to talk about it with experienced people, all you have to do is roam the aisles there.

Being an adoptive parent *is* being a parent. I wipe noses, bottoms, and tears; I endure late bedtimes, early wakeups, throw-ups, and *My Little Pony*. I am *The Mom*; I make my daughter safe. Like every mom, I hold my children's stories with them. With this child, I hold another mom, too, and aunts, uncles, cousins, grandparents, and a father we've never met. Her story will feel to her simple or complicated, I can't say or know or even guess. Sometimes it feels simple and other times complicated to hold this story with her.

Before we adopted a baby, I had no idea that within the parent universe I'd find a whole other tribe, the adoptive mothers, who share in this particular complexity, the one in which another woman entrusts her most precious creation to you. In a way, you're mothering on behalf of yourself *and* another mother. It's an added responsibility, and it's an honor.

When people first told me, "My child, my adopted child, is the biggest gift in my whole life," I got it. I get it. It's just the case. In the midst of daily life, I don't always think about the big words and the big concepts. The day-to-day is family life. Adoption is absolutely part of our family's fabric, not at the outskirts. When I do think about it, I realize it's so woven into our cloth now that we don't necessarily have to tease the threads out all the time. Because of that solid weave, I don't question some of the things I did early on. By now I *know* that as a mom, I'm not less than; I'm not more than; I'm not altruistic. I'm living my life. We're living our lives. *This* is our family.

CONFESSIONS OF A BORN-BAD MOTHER /
JOY LADIN

hOW BAD A MOTHER AM I? So bad that my children call me Daddy.

I was born to be a bad mother. My bad-motherhood is literally written in my genes, in the form of the Y chromosome that waves its helplessly male arms in every cell of my body, waiting futilely to be replaced by the second X chromosome that would transform me from a male-to-female transsexual into a real woman.

During the fifteen years that I lived as a married heterosexual father, the name "Daddy" was an honorific, a public sign of my love for my children and my children's love for me. But even then I felt like a bad mother. No matter how many miles I walked with babies or toddlers strapped to my chest, cradled in my arms, or swaying on my shoulders; no matter how many diapers I changed, meals I cooked, dishes I washed; and no matter how many hours I waited to pee after a long drive in order to meet the endless stream of pent-up childhood demands for food, play, and attention, I could never move the needle on the meter of Good Motherhood, because I wasn't and never would be a mother.

It wasn't my fault that I wasn't a mother. I didn't ask to be born male, and I never wanted the uterus-challenged body I inexplicably found myself inhabiting. But as my wife's body, pregnancy books, and every mention of motherhood reminded me, my XY chromosomes rendered me incapable of either enduring the burdens or achieving the miracles of female reproduction. Menstruation, pregnancy, miscarriage, childbirth, nursing, the suffering they entail, and the courage they demand, were constitutionally beyond me.

But it wasn't just biology that marked me as a bad mother. My maternal inadequacy was a social given whenever I mingled with mothers, which I often did when I took my small children to daycare, preschool, or playgrounds. When mothers were talking mom-to-mom, I couldn't join in without disrupting the conversation, like a shaggy dog bounding up to be petted. Even in the egalitarian college-town venues in which I did pickups, drop offs, playdates, and parties, my biology was my social destiny: I might be recognized by mothers (the ultimate judges) as "a great dad," but the top of the fatherhood scale fell well short of the lowest rung of true motherhood.

Being a dad among moms has its perks, of course. I was praised for even the smallest parental involvement: Look, he changes diapers! Wipes drool! Soothes screaming infants! No matter how equally my wife and I shared family chores, my wife's mothering was constantly being measured against that of her peers, but no one judged me on the quality of our kids' diets or the creativity of their birthday parties. Since the social as well as biological burden of good motherhood always fell squarely on her—despite her feminist critiques and commitments—my wife embraced the children's clothing, feeding, and so on as her personal responsibilities. And since she had been raised female and I had been raised male, we both agreed that she was infinitely more capable than I was of handling aesthetics, details, and planning. Though I did much of the chopping, cooking, and cleaning up, she chose the meal recipes. Even when I dressed the kids, she laid out the clothes—and seemed authentically horrified on the rare occasions when I dared to put together an outfit. Though I did most of the grocery shopping (with children in tow), she assembled the lists I relied on—which meant that she planned all the meals and kept track of everyone's needs and supplies. As the social standard of Good Mothering demanded, she took on the mental work of parenting, from noticing who needed a new toothbrush to evaluating school choices. Per the social definition of good fathering, I "helped," spending hours discussing household concerns as our children multiplied. But we both believed that no matter how mentally capable I might be in my professional life, my father's brain was simply not sharp enough, my grasp of my children's needs simply not clear enough, for me to be entrusted with planning, scheduling, remembering, noticing.

Don't get me wrong. I loved the aspects of parenting that fell to me. To this day, years after living apart from my children, my body aches to feel a small body squirming against it. Had I actually been a man, I probably would have been gratified when mothers, including mine, said I was "so good with the kids"— but this phrase, bestowed as a high compliment on fathers, would be an insult to any mother. A father who's good with kids is considered a great father; a mother who's good with kids is considered . . . a mother. And though I never envied my wife the interminable work of thinking about household concerns, the oft-repeated self-fulfilling prophecy of my male incapacity for it sealed my sense of maternal inadequacy.

But maternal inadequacy represented by being a "good dad" was nothing compared to the disaster that followed my transition to living as a woman. There's no scale of parenting values in which gender transition is a plus—and most non-transexual onlookers consider it a sign of abject, irremediable failure. No matter what I did for or with my children, I was no longer in the running to be considered a good parent of either gender once I started presenting myself as a woman.

My children told me, frequently, that I could never be their mother because they already had one; my eight-year-old daughter shared her opinion that my transition made me a bad role model for my then-fourteen-year-old son. There was even a legal presumption that gender transition made me a bad parent: When my wife filed for divorce, I was subjected to a court investigation to determine if my transition made me a danger to my children. The lengthy psychologist's report officially decided that though transition made me too self-absorbed to be a good parent, I wasn't dangerous because I would do what my therapist told me to do. Though it was my ex who filed for divorce, and my ex who argued that I should have limited contact with my children, the law treated me as a father abandoning his family, a twist on the usual paternal selfishness and incontinence, though in my case it was wearing women's clothing rather than having an affair or gambling that I was putting ahead of my children's needs. Other than a few friends, my therapist, and my attorney, no one seemed to believe that I had delayed transition until it was the only alternative to suicide, and that I had endured years of anguish and isolation because I couldn't bear to leave my children. Like most parents whose transition precipitates divorce, I lost physical custody and was entitled to see my children only three times a week.

Needless to say, at no point in this process was my ex's quality as a parent in question, both because she wasn't transsexual and because, as every court believes, children are better off with their mother. In fact, my transition increased my ex's Good-Mother quotient. My ex was seen as a heroic single mother, bravely soldiering on after the devastating betrayal of their father, a man so feckless he literally wouldn't keep his pants on for the sake of his children. No one knew that she rebuffed my efforts to continue to share the daily work of parenting, though for a while I insisted on vacuuming the house I no longer lived in. Even though my ex had initiated the divorce, everyone knew the breakup was my fault.

But I have never fought harder or suffered more for love of my children than after my new life as a woman won me the gold medal for maternal failure. Like many transsexuals, I felt as though I had been reborn: For the first time in almost fifty years, I walked the world as the person I knew myself to be. Like every newborn, I wanted my miraculous new self to be loved, held, cherished. But that, of course, wasn't how my children saw it. To them, my new self wasn't a miracle; it was a catastrophe that had destroyed their home, their lives, their world. Even today, when new relationships and lives have risen from the rubble, they wish that I—the real, female me—had never been born.

There's nothing unusual about my children's feelings. It's easy for a noncustodial parent in an acrimonious divorce to become demonized, a safe repository for the rage all children feel when adults who should be caring for them inexplicably disrupt their lives. When the reason for such a divorce is gender transition, it's hard for children to distinguish transition from divorce, their trans parent's emergence into the light of day from the shattering of their home. No matter what I did when I was with them, I had utterly failed them as a parent. No matter how they begged, I wouldn't go back to living as a man, or living with their real—they would say only—mother. No matter how they wept when I left, I still left. No matter how much they longed for me, I wasn't there to murmur to them when they had trouble falling asleep, comfort their nightmares, kiss them awake in the morning.

Everything I knew and loved about being their parent had been stripped away; all that was left was showing up. Whenever I had a chance to see them, I did, erasing my fledgling female self by assuming once more the clothes and voice of a man. No matter how broken my heart felt, I gazed with love into their stony faces, gave hugs and kisses that weren't returned, waited patiently for them to look at, talk to, and play with me. I sobbed every time I left them. I hated myself for not being with them, for failing to be able to be the man they mourned and missed, for surviving living apart from them.

I became an unnameable kind of parent, a parent defined wholly by negations: noncustodial, non-male, not a mother, no longer a father, not present enough, not invisible enough, not a danger but definitely not good in any way. No one knew what someone in my position should do or should be; all anyone could tell me, from friends to therapists and rabbis, was that no matter how angry my children were or how much I hurt, I had to be there for them, whenever and however I could. And so I was, day after day, year after year, while new forms of relationships and love grew around the gaping wounds of transition and divorce, which I know will always be there.

Even after five years of healing, I am still in some ways nameless. "Mama" is their mother, their very good mother, and I am—they aren't quite sure. Usually they call me "Daddy" and "he," but sometimes pronouns slip, and recently my older daughter told me that when I referred to myself as "father" in a card I wrote her, it felt wrong and strange. She didn't know what other word to use, because our words and relationships with parents are so deeply enmeshed with gender, there is no name for what I am to her.

But my children know one thing for sure: No matter how I fail as a father or mother, I will love them utterly, and always.

THE IMPOSSIBILITY OF THE GOOD BLACK MOTHER /
T. F. CHARLTON

COULD TELL YOU...

I could tell you that I don't want to be burdened by the expectation that I should be a Good Mother. That I don't want to be defined by my relationship to my child, papered over, or perpetually obligated to be a blank slate of all-encompassing, self-denying nurture and devotion.

I could tell you that I don't want to be seen, to be treated, as the (never quite) Good (enough) Mother. As best as I can tell from professional feminists who are supposed to be in the know, this seems to be the Proper Feminist thing to do.

I could tell you that. It wouldn't be entirely true.

I am a mother. For good or ill, it does define me. Mother isn't all that I am, but it's a 24/7 gig. I am all the mother my child has, and neither her life nor mine will be the same for it.

I am a dark-skinned Black mother, a relatively young one, raising my daughter in predominantly white spaces, at least for now. I'm not infrequently mistaken for a high school student, despite being thirty. On most days, I look the part of the harried graduate student I used to be, rocking a jeans and t-shirt look with the occasional oversized sweatshirt. I have long abandoned my half-hearted attempts to conform even loosely to the wardrobe expected of women of my age and class.

I know how this looks to many people.

To be young and Black in America is to know you're the last person the mainstream wants to have reproduce, much less succeed as a parent. Indeed, in a culture of white supremacy, many institutions invest considerable effort and resources into preventing Black women from becoming mothers, and into ensuring that we have as little structural support as possible when we do.

To be young and Black in America is the knowledge that if you do become a parent, and a mother especially, your parenthood will be viewed as illegitimate, literally and symbolically. And that people will make assumptions and inferences about all sorts of things: the circumstances under which your children were conceived, your relationship to the other parent, your competence as a parent, your care for your children's welfare.

I could never be the Good Mother; I knew all this long before I had a child. But had I not, the experience of parenting my daughter under the appraising eye of white privilege and supremacy would quickly have disabused me of any illusions that I could be one.

The myth I contend with is not that of the Good Mother, but that of the Bad Black Mother. It's a myth that renders my motherhood at turns invisible and suspect. It's a myth that leaves me with an uneasy desire to be seen as the Good Mother.

The encounters that overtly challenge the legitimacy of my Black motherhood are countless. The unthinking curiosity about whether my light-skinned, curly-haired, biracial daughter is "mine" or not.

The questions about "what" she is, as though she's some strange, unidentifiable breed of dog.

Often as not, the questions come from other people of color. One Ethiopian store clerk, after asking if I'm Abby's mother, marvels at how light she is, tells me my husband's genes must have "won out" over mine.

The Bangladeshi convenience store owner around the corner has forgotten at least three times now that he's already asked me if David and I are married. On one occasion, he regales me with a tale of a Black friend who has half a dozen children with multiple women. "I think this is not good," he says. I wonder what this has to do with me.

Across from the convenience store, I'm dropped off by one of the moms from our daughter's daycare, a white woman. She's seen me walking Abby to school from time to time, and generously offers me a ride. We make small talk about work, and how we like the daycare. As I'm about to step out of the car, she asks about Abby's dad, "And is your husband, um, partner, uh, boyfriend . . . is he in the picture?"

It's a strange question; I'm unsure how to answer. Part of me wants to appreciate that the possibility of my not being married is being acknowledged. But I'm keenly aware that my race, and perhaps her assumptions about my partner's race, are probably the main reasons this even occurs to her. And of course, my family situation is hardly the concern of someone I've only just met.

I'm annoyed by her presumption, but I'm also annoyed at myself for feeling compelled to answer an intrusive question, for feeling the need to make it clear that I am, in fact, married. I don't want this stereotype of me as a Black mother to go unchallenged, but I also don't want to give the slightest impression that being a single Black mother is shameful. Time is short, and I'm on the spot. I say something about my husband being a hands-on dad. It feels inadequate.

A block down is the martial arts studio where Abby takes Tae Kwon Do classes. I take her most days, but every once in a while she goes with her dad. It's a good fit for her. The class gives her some needed routine and discipline, and she loves being around the teachers and her fellow students.

It's a Wednesday night; Abby is getting a goodbye hug from one of her instructors, an older white woman. I'm just thinking how glad I am that we signed Abby up for the class, how grateful I am that she has positive adult role models like this teacher. The teacher turns to me and asks, "Who was that man who came with Abby to class last night?"

I'm flabbergasted, and I feel certain it shows on my face. "Um, my husband?" (I immediately wonder why I say this, rather than "Her dad.")

She tells me she was sure David had some connection to her, since they came together. She just likes to make sure *her* kids are okay. As though I wouldn't know who takes my child to class. As though I might be in the habit of letting my daughter fall into the care of strange men. As though it's up to her, a new acquaintance, to confirm that I'm living up to my parental responsibilities.

The odd exchange can be explained only by an assumption on her part that David couldn't possibly be a Black woman's partner, or a Black girl's dad. That David is Abby's dad would be the natural assumption under most circumstances; most children at the studio are brought by their parents, a few by other adult relatives. Abby's climbing all over her father and calling him "daddy" would also be a decisive clue for most people. But race privilege has a funny way of keeping people from seeing the obvious; people see what they expect to see.

This is not all of my existence as a Black mother; it doesn't wholly define me, or how my mothering is perceived. But it is a part of my story. Histories and meanings are mapped on to my skin by a culture that holds my inferiority as indisputable dogma. In the pediatrician's office, in the grocery store, on the neighborhood streets I call my own, my motherhood is always potentially suspect.

This is patriarchy: entitlement to the scrutiny and policing of bodies that are, or are perceived as, female. As mothers, we belong to a global sorority of women laboring under expectations that our parenting be open to any and all interrogation. But as with any oppression, we don't share this burden evenly, or identically.

The mother who chafes under expectations that she is, or must want to be, all the Good Mother is—married to the father of her children, nurturing to the point of self-abnegation, a model of middle class domesticity—she tells one story. To some degree, I can empathize, since I'm a daughter of Nigerian and Christian fundamentalist cultures that often demand selfless childbearing and childrearing of women.

Still, the images projected on me as I walk my neighborhood streets are not of the Good Mother. No, they are of the Black welfare queen, the baby mama, of women maligned and demonized as everything a mother should not be, foil and shadow to the Good (White) Mother.

The curiosity that strangers are so often eager to satisfy when they see me with my daughter is profoundly shaped by these images. Am I the babysitter? The nanny? Or that perennial bogeywoman of white family values—the teen mother—whose sexuality and reproduction flout the bounds of heteronormative marriage? People dearly love to know.

There is no single story of motherhood, or the misogynist tales patriarchy tells about mothers. The myth of the Good Mother is built on the back of scorn for mothers like me. There's no reckoning with this myth, no challenging it, without recognizing this. Being expected to embody "traditional" femininity, it turns out, is its own strange sort of privilege.

I am far from the first to observe the following assessment: portrayals of "respectable" Black motherhood are so rare as to be "revolutionary."[1] They are dangerously seductive.[2]

When I respond to questions about my motherhood, am I simply challenging notions that I cannot be a Good Mother, or falling for the

---

[1] Tamara Winfrey Harris, "A Black Mom-in-Chief is Revolutionary: What White Feminists Get Wrong about Michelle Obama," *Clutch Magazine,* Sept. 11, 2012, http://www.clutchmagonline.com/2012/09/a-black-mom-in-chief-is-revolutionary-what-white-feminist-get-wrong-about-michelle-obama/
Deesha Philyaw, "Michelle Obama, Mom-in-Chief," *Bitch*, April 20, 2009, http://bitchmagazine.org/post/michelle-obama-mom-in-chief

[2] Tamara Winfrey Harris, "No Disrespect," *Bitch* 55 (Summer 2012):32.

siren song of "proper" Black motherhood made in the image of polite, white-washed femininity? The lines are blurry. Respectability may be resistance, but it is neither solidarity with my sisters, nor liberation for any of us.

Liberation is confronting my own internalized shame and anxieties about justifying myself to whiteness. It's disrupting the very notion of illegitimate motherhood and the harm it does.

I, too, have privileges. I've experienced medical discrimination, but my ability to plan my family and maintain my health doesn't depend on services constantly threatened because poor mothers of color are seen as undeserving. Stereotypes that fuel curiosity and judgment about my mothering don't compromise my material safety and well-being as they do for Black mothers who are single or depend on government assistance.

I worry about raising a Black girl in a world where girls of color, especially, are always "asking for" whatever violence befalls them. Being around police makes my pulse race and my steps quicken. I worry that someday my brothers—both six-foot-plus Black men— or my cousins, or my dad, might find themselves being Black and male at the wrong end of a cop's gun. To be Black and a mother in America means sharing in the collective fear that "our children will be dragged from a car and shot down in the street," only to be met with white indifference.[3]

But this fear is more of a daily, present reality for some than it is for others. I don't live under a state of constant police surveillance and occupation, or pervasive state and domestic violence, as so many Black mothers and their families do.

Yet this structural violence against Black girls, women, and families is enabled and perpetuated by the same ingrained disdain for Black motherhood that underlies the micro-aggressions I experience.

———

[3] Audre Lorde, "Age, Race, Class, and Sex: Women Redefining Difference," *Sister Outsider: Essays and Speeches* (Berkeley: Crossing Press, 2007), 119.

These very images are used to justify systematic violence against Black communities, and indifference to this violence.

It's precisely for this reason that I examine my own response to questions about my motherhood. Why am I sometimes quick to clarify that David is my husband? In responding to racist and sexist assumptions, do I inadvertently or subconsciously distance myself from *those* Black mothers?

If I'm honest with myself, I want to be seen as a Good Mother. But if my aim in disrupting the stereotype of the Bad Black Mother is simply to establish myself, and Black women like me, as good and respectable mothers, I am only working to secure some small benefit of white supremacy for myself.

If I'm honest with myself, I have to confront my own shame and defensiveness in response to racist and misogynist stereotypes. I have to process the ways in which society places pressures on Black mothers like me, who appear to conform to classed and raced heteronormative expectations, to shun solidarity with Black women whose motherhood is less "respectable."

I could tell you that I don't want to be seen as the Good Mother. This would be a lie, and an unnecessary one. Part of my struggle is to challenge the notion that good motherhood cannot exist in bodies like mine.

But I can tell you something I want even more: a world where respect is seen as inherent in humanity itself and therefore the rights of all mothers, and all people, are universally respected. A world where no litmus test is required for us to see worth and dignity in the beautiful mess of singularities and complexities that we are.

This is better than being acknowledged as a Good Mother: to be seen as a mother and fully human at once. This is liberation.

NOT YOUR AVERAGE
TEEN MOTHER /
ELIZABETH CROSSEN

IT'S RUSH HOUR ON FRIDAY evening, and the El train bounces on its tracks as it moves deeper into West Philadelphia, becoming less suffocating as it relieves itself of riders. Sitting in two of the fuzzy blue seats behind me are two small, giggly children, a boy and a girl. My heart aches in my chest as I watch them, their playful innocence a familiar trigger these days as I navigate the world away from my own. They're splayed across the seats, playfully teasing each other like a big brother and little sister would. Their mother is sitting across the aisle from them, so absorbed by her phone that I am unconvinced the children are actually in her care. As the kids break into a tickle fight, bouncing and screeching with delight, the mother, clearly annoyed, jerks her head toward them and yells at them to be quiet. She is quickly consumed by her phone again, and the children play on. I study her as this pattern continues: she ignores them, they play rambunctiously as children do, and she snaps at them to behave. One stop before mine, they prepare to exit. The mother screams at them about empty juice boxes, and stray crumbs in the aisle. They are not quiet enough for her, they are not moving quickly enough for her. Her impatience and annoyance is the behavior of a mother who doesn't know what it means to be without them. Her irritation chafes at me—but I also understand it. That was me once, flustered, exhausted, irritable, and jumpy from trying to navigate public spaces alone with two young children, myself barely an adult by then at nineteen. Had time and distance really molded me into a fresh-faced twenty-something, with my shiny new degree and underpaying first "real" job after college, disguising me as an anonymous voyeur, knee-jerking judgment at an overworked mother just trying to get home? Was I *really* daring myself to believe that I was doing it any better? The doors slide open, and the frazzled mom moves onto the platform, a child's hand gripped firmly in each of hers. The doors close and they are gone.

I had just completed my sophomore year of high school when I found out I was pregnant. I had been on the pill since I was fourteen, so it was a shock. To make matters worse, I had just broken up with my boyfriend, so it was hard to tell him. It took two more tests and a trip to Planned Parenthood to convince him it was real. He was in denial and I was completely petrified. Without a compass to direct me, I relied heavily on the expectations of others. Their unwavering advice was to have an abortion, but what *I* really wanted was someone to validate my own desire: to keep this child, but I was too paralyzed with fear to admit it. So I went through the motions, navigated the steps toward an abortion, had the appointment, fought off the protesters at the clinic, and resigned myself to the inevitable. The deeper part of me resisted with a ferocity that ultimately won over. I cancelled the procedure and insisted that I would carry my son to term. There was a brief flirtation with giving the child up for adoption, under the pressure of others, including my boyfriend, but in that time, as my first child grew in my body, I cultivated the courage to announce my intent. I wanted to keep this child and raise it.

I wanted to be a mother.

The immense joy and gratitude I had for my new baby boy clouded the overwhelming loneliness that accompanied being a mother at seventeen. My friends were not interested in continuing a relationship with me now that I was a twosome. My boyfriend returned to school a week after our son was born and I finished my classes from home. Hours became days, and days became months of sitting on the couch in my parents' cavernous living room, nursing and playing with my sweet boy, waiting for someone to come home and interact with me. I had been told all throughout my pregnancy how difficult and impossible caring for a child would be, but that was not how my life as a new mother proved to be. Caring for my son was fairly easy—he was such a joyful, mild-mannered baby, and I relished every moment with him. And yet, in looking back on it, I wondered at how I could feel at once so empty and yet so fulfilled. How I could pour myself into another human being, leaving me without any reserves for myself. It took years to really understand that dichotomy—when you are in so deep, it is impossible to see anything that is not immediately in front of you.

Rushing off the train, I use my small frame to maneuver through the mass of people moving at once toward their next destination, cattle squeezing through the livestock gate. Gulping air, I slide on to the calloused leather seats of the Norristown High Speed Line. Journeying from my awkward desk jockey post at a nonprofit in far away Camden, New Jersey, I am finally in the last twenty minutes of my commute to my boyfriend's apartment in King of Prussia. The icy February sky now black, the enormous window is a mirror. In that reflection, I challenge the woman staring back at me to explore where her criticisms had come from. The truth, not so much deeply hidden as it is painful, was that I could no longer understand how the day-to-day, second-to-second stresses of raising children would make you want to silence their laughter, make them vanish into the scenery for just a little while, so you could be someone like me: an anonymous, child-free woman venturing out to spend the evening with her handsome boyfriend.

Instead, living without my two sons has turned such memories nostalgic.

The old feeling of swimming in a shark tank without oxygen that comes from tending constantly to the needs of two little people is now supplanted by the constant anxiety of missing them, worrying about them, wondering about them. Anxiety that could swamp me with such force, I would never stand again.

I was nineteen when my second son was born on a hazy blue morning in June. Their father began school that fall, so rather than continue working and even enrolling myself, I stayed home with the boys. My desires, passions, and hopes were eclipsed by the needs of two small children, fighting to keep the three of us entertained in a small college town built to be a playground for its enormous student population. With a full course load and a job delivering pizza—often until three or four in the morning—their dad was rarely home, and when he was, he would become furious that I had not cleaned the house thoroughly enough, that he was too exhausted for dishes and laundry. He had no frame of reference to understand, nor could I articulate to him, that if I could sprout six more arms, there would never be another dirty dish left in the sink; that I would never have to spend an hour getting from the driveway to the front door of our apartment because our two-year-old would become a willful noodle at some point along the thirty-yard walk, and I couldn't tote his infant brother and wrestle him along too. There were days when I would get dressed in the morning, sometimes putting on jewelry, wondering what or who I was doing it for. Perhaps it was just a way to make me feel meaningful, even normal. The tension and loneliness would gnaw at what I could only guess was my soul, spending every day waiting for . . . something. Whatever it was, it never came.

When I started college at twenty-one, the boys were four and two. My twenty-credit course load and thirty-five-hour work week undoubtedly could make a zombie out of most, even those with titanium work ethics. But for me, it was like seeing the ocean for the first time. The world became infinitely bigger; it gave me such a strong, solid sense of self and purpose. At last, I had something in my life that was mine entirely! The boys' father and I ended our relationship during this time, and my children stayed with me on weekdays. Our lives became a daily cycle of hurdles: from getting up and fed and dressed and off to our respective schools on time, to the day's end, when my patience wore thin as I willed the hours to pass to the boys' bedtime so I could study and write papers, often all night long. Dinners at hyperspeed, stories read as though I were set on fast-forward. Every Friday, I could not get them into their father's care fast enough so I could live my uninhibited weekend social life. I was frantic to finish school in three years, to get into the best graduate program, to make a life for the boys and me that would ease some of this manic rushing. Everything felt so fucking important, so urgent and necessary, and I was so desperate to get from point A to point B, so desperate for moments to myself.

What is so painfully ironic is that all of my work, all of those sacrificed moments with my sons, was not in vain. I did graduate in three years, got into a top graduate program, and now work at a career-track job while continuing my schooling. Everything I set out to achieve, I did. All while having ten times the pressure and obligation of my peers. None of it gives me any real sense of accomplishment or satisfaction, because in many ways, I am emptier than I have ever been.

And here's the truth of me alone in that train car: I left my children behind in order to attend graduate school, in order to take this job. "It's temporary," I tell and retell myself, in an attempt to reassure myself—and, more importantly, them. "It's just this one year . . ." I am a broken record stuck repeating one refrain. But in spite of these internal placations, I know my sweet little boys, those innocent people whom I brought into this world, are hurt and confused and angry and scared. I worry that they'll believe everyone leaves, that growing up will mean being without anyone in the world to love you. Will this be a pain they carry through their lives? Will they understand one day why Mama had to go for a little while . . . and forgive me for it? To know I'm doing it not simply out of ambition, but so they don't have to struggle to pay for college like their father and I did, or sit in their apartments starving for days, wondering how they will cover the rent, pay to get to work, or buy new shoes when their only pair have worn out. And will they wonder, like I do sometimes, whether this time spent "getting my shit in order for our greater good" is worth this black hole of time apart? Is it worth their pain and worth the futile dance I do every day to suppress the anxieties of missing them and worrying about them: Are they ok? Are they safe and well-fed? Are they lonely, sad? Are they being driven around safely enough, sleeping in a locked house, going to public bathrooms with an adult standing outside waiting?

Are they going to be okay after this is over?

The crowd on the high-speed line thins as my stop approaches, the lights of cars jammed on I-76 below periodically provide hints to how close I am getting. Another day done, another week, all without much distinction from one to the next. I allow myself to breathe, to reconcile that the judgments I held for that woman were so futile and misplaced; she is no different from me—we are just mothers trying to do our best, in our myriad forms—for better or worse. Who am I to judge? There will undoubtedly be a time again when I want nothing but personal space—to be an individual, a woman, not just mother—and I hope that I can look back on this time now and remember how I felt the bittersweet yearning to press my face into those children's hair, and my urge to scold that mother for not cherishing every second she had with them. I have traded the claustrophobia of everyday mothering for a life spent living so closely with myself, that every day is now a cycle of coming home, searching for company, for a drink, for a person to fill the faults and rifts of a life that I can hardly recognize anymore without my children to define it. And this is why I cherish my small pockets of time with them, when they come.

I step off the train and spot my boyfriend waiting in his warm car. He reaches to open the door for me as I approach. We begin to make the three-hour drive to visit those wonderful boys; they will be sleeping soundly when we arrive, but we will have the next two days to be a family, to make up for all that we lose between visits. And that will get us through for a little while, and maybe gain some restored faith that we can get through this and somehow be okay.

ALL THE SINGLE LADIES /
JENNIFER BAUMGARDNER

t
he summer of 2007, when my son Skuli was almost three, I flew back early from a trip to Fargo so I could attend a party for Jenny and Sara Jane, two friends of mine who were celebrating their five-year relationship. Jenny and Sara Jane were a decade younger than I, Smith graduates with great style and even more beautiful politics. I was excited to go to their ceremony, which struck me as risky and brave. Their families weren't always comfortable and on board with their daughter's sexuality. Having everyone convene for this celebration of a gay relationship was, to my mind, a big deal. I was hungry for examples of alternative family-making, having logged nearly three years as a single mom by choice.

I was used to traveling alone, but that didn't make it any more pleasant when things went awry. Skuli was easy, but it wasn't like I had another adult to carry the bags, figure out the missed connection, or help clean up the milk vomit after the bumpy flight—things which happened with annoying regularity. It was a blazing hot July afternoon when we arrived at JFK after a long flight. I threw our bags in Skuli's Sit 'n' Stroll, a car seat/stroller combo that I used in airports like a wheelbarrow when I traveled with him. Carrying him on one hip, I slogged out to the long-term parking lot. Our car, a 17-year-old red Honda Civic, shimmered in the heat. *This isn't good,* I thought, heart sinking, because one of the many quirks of this vehicle (passed down from mother to sister to me) was that it wouldn't start when parked in direct sunlight. I fastened Skuli's car seat into the cauldron of the backseat and turned the ignition, praying it would turn over. Nothing. I waited two minutes. Still nothing. Again—

"We should call someone to help us," Skuli offered from his microwave oven perch. He was good at intuiting our next step.

I called someone (JFK Roadside Assistance, maybe?) and soon a young guy arrived to jump our battery. "It's not the battery," I said, wishing I had thought to pack snacks and a water bottle for Skuli. "This car doesn't start in heat. I have to wait until sundown."

"It's the battery, Ma'am," the car guy said. After ten more minutes of needless jumping, hope, and disappointment, he offered to drive us in his tow truck to the nearest garage. Feeling a familiar financial panic, I mentally calculated the cost of this crisis—$60 for tow, $50 for car service home, God knows how much to "fix" the car (i.e., let car come to room temperature)—and wondered if witnessing Jenny and Sara Jane's commitment was worth the expense. I decided it was. We got home in time for me to shower and change, drop Skuli at his dad's for the night, and head to the party.

On a Brooklyn rooftop that night, drinking restoratively, I met Sara Jane's mom. A former nurse with great bone structure, frosted blonde hair, and a mini dress, her whole body vibed, "Be surprised that I have two adult daughters." She was a former single mother, and as we continued to drink and listen to the iPod playlist Jenny and Sara Jane had selected for this night, she prodded me for stories about my life.

After each story, she'd shake her head and say, "Be selfish, Jen. You've *got* to be selfish."

I was used to getting unsolicited advice about my life, especially from people I considered to be less than knowledgeable. Some of it I gratefully accepted, like the offers to come over for Sunday dinner, and the used baby equipment my friends were always finding for me. Sometimes, though, I sensed not so much helpfulness but pity. I mean, I felt bad for some of *them*, what with their unhappy marriages and wilting sex lives, but I got the feeling that they used me to feel better about their own lives. "I know it must be so hard," these friends would say, flattening me into a stereotype with their sympathy faces (furrowed brow, lips pressed into a droopy frown) and their "Does Skuli have male role models? Is his dad, you know, *involved?*" concerns.

The truth is, it *was* hard. I woke up in the middle of the night worried about bills, anxious that I'd have coverage for Skuli while I was working. I brought him to parties with me not because he loved hanging out at adult's houses at 11:30 PM, but because it was that or never socialize. But . . . I was *happy*. I'd never felt so much love and independence at once.

Back at the party, I attempted to respond to Sara Jane's mom. As a single mother, I was not self*ish*—that suffix "ish" connoting something gross or halfway. It's more like I was self-full. It was definitely a time in my life in which I had to rely on myself more than ever before, and yet my life was very rich with other people: Christine dropping by on the way home from work because I've conveyed that friends are always welcome, saying yes to spontaneous invitations to the Bronx Zoo because Skuli and I don't have to negotiate anyone else's schedule, New Year's Eves with Amy and Peter, sleepovers at Gillian's because we only need one bed.

The nuclear family, I noted, was a more *closed* home, electrons orbiting around the nucleus of the dinner table, ordered primarily by the schedules of its members. In my single-lady status, my home was open. I controlled the doors and I wanted people to come in. My friends and family showed up for me all of the time. My sister Jessica, happily married and also a mother, marveled at how much help from friends and family I marshaled. "I guess I'm not afraid to ask," I said, attempting to analyze the discrepancy. "And people assume I need it, of course, which is kind of humiliating."

"Not as humiliating as needing it even though you have a partner," Jessica responded.

Clearly, Jessica wasn't one of the condescending types, but I gravitated toward single parent friends after Skuli was born. We were the ones who always dropped our kids late at school and got stern, condescending looks from the teachers. We brought our children to cocktail parties and readings, because it was that or we couldn't go. The single moms had scuffed shoes; our roots grown out from a little too much time between hair appointments. Superficially, we were more bedraggled, but we were also a really sturdy, actualized crew. Alan (as a man, an honorary single mom) was a poet, professor, and art critic who kept a perfect house for himself and Sophie. Sixty-something Merle owned the largest abortion clinic in the country and became a self-made millionaire before adopting Sasha from Siberia. Liliana had left Poland, escaped her abusive husband, and was raising Anna and Alex while working full time and going back to school. Sally wanted the baby but not the bad-boy baby daddy, and was raising her son exactly how she wanted—with organic food, no sugar, and lots of travel. Lorraine had three children, two exes, three enormously successful salons, and, in spite of being dyslexic, had written a book. We shared a common currency—the bracing combination of independence and terror. The independence was precious—"I get to write three nights a week," as Alan would often say—but it was the terror (Food on table! Clothes on kid! Insurance! Tuition!) that kept us motivated.

I felt lonely some days—the obvious ones, like Valentine's Day and Mother's Day—but the other days I felt this magical self-reliance. "Trust thyself," as Emerson wrote, "every heart vibrates to that iron string." I had ample opportunity to learn to trust myself, and maybe opportunity (also known as necessity) is just what one needs. Single parenthood was good for me, but people tend to feel bad for the children of single mothers, too, I noted. The assumption was that boys needed a role model and girls needed to know their dad would love and protect them. Heading into the subway one day, I was struggling with the stroller (Skuli in it and heavy) and my bags. Out of the corner of my eye, I saw a teen thug walking toward me with a menacingly blank look on his face and his pants drooped. He leaned over, picked up my carriage and, without a word, carried Skuli down the two flights of stairs to the subway platform. I sputtered a thank you. He looked me in the eye and said in a soft voice, "I was raised by a single mom, Ma'am."

My friend Amy was raised by a single mom. When she turned thirty, her friends made a book for her, each of us taking a page to extol her work ethic, dance ability, and generosity. Her mother's page had a snapshot of the two of them, taken when Amy was about five and her mother was in her young twenties. The photographer was behind the two. Her mother is pointing at a flower right in front of them, showing it to Amy. And Amy is pointing up and away, to something that her mom can't even see. She wrote that it wasn't the most flattering photo of the two of them, but it was a good example of their relationship. The caption Amy's mother wrote was "We make a good team. We make a good team."

The fact that she wrote it twice slayed me, but I was most struck by seeing my tough, confident, sunny friend cry as she read the words. I think Amy knew that thing that I know and that Skuli knows and that all of the single moms know: the joy, beauty, and hard-earned satisfaction of being a good team. Days before that awful moment at JFK when my car wouldn't start, we visited my cousins at their lake cabin in Minnesota. Their house was crawling with kids and my cousin and her husband appeared to have an attractive, invitingly healthy relationship. The kids swam and hunted for minnows and played with toy cars. When it was time to leave, Skuli threw himself on the ground and cried, "No, I won't go! I *belong* here."

He had done the same thing a few weeks earlier at Amy's house, at which there was the same appealing constellation of happy and fun parents, cool toys, and siblings. Both times, I felt a chill course through me, because his response struck me as maybe true and certainly insightful. Not that he needed to have two parents, but there was something about the joviality and regularity of that home that either vibrated with what he knew about other people and missed in his own life—or it just felt right in some meaningful way that his three-year-old self needed to assert.

To me, it hurt, because I knew I belonged with him but I didn't belong there—and I wanted him to believe, as I did, that we were lucky that things had worked out as they did, that our lives were unique and wonderful. Was I just being selfish?

"Be selfish"—these words echoed in my brain the summer Skuli was three. What did it mean? Was it selfish to stay a unit of two, because Skuli would have to shoulder the burdens of my aging alone? Or was it selfish to have a love life when I had a young child who needed me? I could see it both ways and many more.

It may have just been a coincidence, but after that "selfish" conversation, I got my mojo back. By mojo, I mean my sexual self. I began dating again later that month, and within a few weeks I met the man that would become the father of my second child and, later, this same man—BD—became my husband. Skuli has thrived in our nuclear family, stricter and more constant than what he knew before. I wonder sometimes if he remembers our former way of being. Will he know to help a struggling mom with her stroller in ten years?

"We don't spend as much time together," Skuli told me one day, while walking home from school. We were holding hands and he had been telling me about his life in an alternate universe he calls Boneland. "You spend a lot of time with BD now."

I squeezed his hand.

"Remember when we were just the two of us," Skuli asked, "and we'd sleep together in the same bed?"

"I do remember," I said. "We made a good team, Skuli."

We made a good team.

THE WAY IT'S SUPPOSED TO BE /
KRISTEN OGANOWSKI

PREGNANT WOMEN ARE SUBJECT TO a litany of things that they are "supposed" to do, or ways that they are "supposed" to be, some more legitimate and well-intentioned than others: You're not supposed to drink alcohol.

You're not supposed to change the cat's litter box.

You're not supposed to consume too much caffeine.

You're not supposed to eat soft cheeses, or rare steak, even if you have nightly dreams about diving headfirst into a dark-pink filet mignon slathered in bleu cheese.

You're not supposed to feel anything but angelic and undying love toward your fetus, even if your darling unborn baby keeps you up at night with heartburn and wicked kicks to the ribs.

You're not supposed to work too much, or relax too much, or exercise too much, or eat too much, or stress out too much.

You're not supposed to be too fat or too thin, too active or too sedentary.

And you're not supposed to announce your pregnancy "too early." At least not until after the first trimester (and the greatest risk of miscarriage) is over because, you know, if you do miscarry *then you'll have to tell everyone.* And that's supposed to be awkward and terrible.

Or at least it's supposed to make you *feel* awkward and terrible.

In February 2011, ten weeks and one day into a planned and very much wanted pregnancy, that's exactly what happened to me. I suffered a miscarriage.

In the morning, in the bathroom, I noticed a shock of pink on my tissue.

The spot was small, mucousy, tinged with the color of the heart-shaped candies that people would be passing out to their Valentines throughout the day.

"Bloody show," the books call it. A sign that labor is about to begin. A message that your body is ready to birth your baby.

Except that I was far from the estimated due date, which stretched out seven months ahead of me.

In that moment, with the shock of pink before me, I knew that I would not be "birthing" or "having" a baby by the day's end.

I would be losing my baby.

I had already announced my pregnancy to family, friends, neighbors, and to the thousands of strangers who'd read my pregnancy resource blog, Birthing Beautiful Ideas, when I was a mere five weeks pregnant. In addition to that medium-rare, bleu cheese-slathered steak I had eaten, this was yet another Thing That I Wasn't Supposed to Do. And now I had to make the presumably awkward and terrible announcement that I was no longer pregnant.

"Sorry, folks, there's nothing to see here. Move along, move along, nothing's happened."

Though I knew of no specific guidelines for how to proceed

through my loss, most social cues told me this: You render miscarriage invisible. You speak about it in hushed tones. You don't bring it up, you don't ask about it.

You move along, as if nothing ever happened.

By noon that day, the certainty of my loss had become apparent.

The menstrual-like cramps. The rhythmic ebb and flow of a uterine contraction. The indubitable, primordial signal to the brain that this is it.

The sensations of labor.

I straddled between territory that was wild and frightening and feelings that were strangely familiar. It was a death, but it felt like birth. The way I rocked on hands and knees, the way that I arched my hips toward the ceiling, struggling to find a position that would relieve the cramp strangling my lower abdomen.

I hearkened back to the words that my midwives had spoken to me just hours before, words that as a professional doula, I'd spoken to others myself. Words I understood, but which I didn't want associated with me in this way. Not yet.

"When this gets intense later on . . ."

"Ten weeks along . . . so this might feel like a mini-labor . . . not as intense, you won't feel the same pressure, but intense in its own right."

"When the baby . . . the tissue . . . right before you pass . . ."

"I can be there to help you through this, any time, day or night . . . just call me."

They had spoken in the gentle and cryptic code that I knew all too well: that way of communicating to someone (without making the person scared out of their minds) that "this pain is going to get more intense; there is still a rugged path to travail; this thing, you know, might hurt like hell."

In an odd way, I felt empowered that I could do this physically demanding thing—that I was able to experience it like this.

But I also felt broken. Wilted. Defeated.

I had lost my baby.

And now I had to tell everyone.

The morning after my miscarriage was the first morning in six weeks that I had woken up knowing that I was "not pregnant."

I felt empty. And uncertain.

Specifically, I felt uncertain about how and whether to share my news. Not just with family and friends but also with my blog, which had this amorphous, largely unknown audience whose reactions to this news I had no way of gauging.

Complicating matters further, I had written weekly accounts of this pregnancy ever since those two pink lines appeared on the pregnancy test. Surely my blog audience would notice if I suddenly stopped with the pregnancy updates—if I simply moved on, as if nothing happened, just like I was "supposed" to do.

At this point, I didn't know *what* I was supposed to do.

Somewhere in the midst of this uncertainty, I decided to live my miscarriage out loud and on my blog. I talked about what we're not "supposed" to talk about: the way miscarriage looked, the way it felt, the complex emotions that arose from the loss. I did it without shame or embarrassment. I revealed my experience to the world and proclaimed that this, too, was a way to cope with pregnancy loss: that suffering in silence, within the walls of my home, was not the only way to have a miscarriage.

My body, which had surely known of its loss far before I was aware of it, was well into its return to its pre-pregnant state.

My breasts had already begun to deflate, like two balloons slowly hissing out the air left inside them.

The tiny baby bump that had appeared just the week before was also vanishing, crawling in and downward with the descent of my uterus.

My five-year-old son, upon hugging his arms around my waist, even made note of how my belly "wasn't so big with the baby anymore."

It had never occurred to me how each time we hugged, his head must have rested right where my tummy was growing. That he might have noticed those first few days of growth and change even more than I did.

I might have thought that such immediate changes would intensify my grief, leaving me with one more image or string of words or intrusive thought to trigger one more round of crying.

But instead, I took these changes as evidence of nature's grace, of my body's kindness.

I didn't want to look or feel pregnant if I wasn't.

I didn't want to be reminded that those breasts wouldn't be nursing in September, that the bump wouldn't bulge with the pace of the baby once growing inside of me.

I simply felt more comfortable sitting in that place of pregnancy loss. Just resting for a moment in the loss itself. Because I wasn't yet prepared to peer around that curtain that separated the space between what came before and what was present: to think too long and hard about the fact that I had spent the last few weeks being pregnant and then, suddenly, I was not.

Perhaps it was evidence of my mind's grace and kindness.

Though I was by no means the first person to do it, I challenged the idea that the "good" pregnant woman keeps quiet when she loses a pregnancy, and that the Good Mother hides the loss from her other children and carries on with work and family obligations as if nothing happened.

I wrote about the peaks and valleys of my moods.

I wrote about my fluctuating ability to be an active and present parent to my two older children as I processed my loss.

I wrote about how I welcomed the opportunity to have someone take my kids for the day so that I could just sit on my couch eating pancakes, watching bad television, and simply *grieve*.

I even went on to write about the trepidation with which I approached the thought of "trying to get pregnant again."

I exposed the messiness of what it was like *for me* to lose a baby.

And in doing so, I discovered a challenge to the belief that a miscarriage announcement is inherently awkward and terrible.

For soon, I discovered not only mountains of compassion and support but also scores of friends, family, and blog readers who'd all had miscarriages.

"Me too."

"*Me too.*"

"Five times before. *Me too.*"

"Just last week. *Me too.*"

"I'm so sorry. *Me too.*"

And many of them had suffered their loss in silence. Alone. Living under the burden of what one is "supposed" to do when a pregnancy is lost.

Some thanked me for sharing my story, and my vulnerability, and my imperfection, in the way that I did. Some found it healing. Some found it reassuring. Some found that it made them feel a little less lonely.

And many wished that they, too, had been able to share their own story during their time of loss.

I decided then and there that shrouding pregnancy loss in hushed tones and invisibility is not something any woman should feel she is supposed to do. Instead, by sharing our stories of loss, we are helping light the path out of the forest for others who come behind us.

Strength through sisterhood.

That, I decided, is something we are supposed to do.

PART V

"NO GOOD" MAMA

JOINT PARENTING /
PAULINE ABRAHAM

OTHER'S DAY, 2012. My three-year-old son and I sit in the cool dark of a local theater while a fairy-winged folk band plays and kids dance at the front of the stage with their entire bodies, the room pulsing with clapping and giggling. I pass my son a tiny box of Goldfish crackers; he leans against me and munches contentedly, taking it all in. I feel tension slide magically from my skin. We are together, and it is the first time he's stopped talking all weekend.

I am thrilled. He is enchanted. I am high.

It had been a beast of a weekend. My partner was out of town for work. It was the middle of an uncharacteristic heat wave. And the kid was in rare form—demanding, willful, back-talking, dog-hitting, nap-refusing form. The only things that had come out of my mouth since 7:00 AM Saturday had been threats and punishments, and by Sunday afternoon I couldn't stand the sound of either my own voice or that of the miniature tyrant demanding more *Yo Gabba Gabba* and starting every question with a mournfully drawn-out "Whyyyy?" (Just a sampling of things I heard myself say: "If you do that, there will be no dessert tonight." "Put it down." "DOWN." "In the bath, or we'll only read two books." "REALLY?" "One book." "NO BOOKS.")

And so I do the thing I usually only do after he's gone to bed for the night: I fire up a little bowl of the pot my husband keeps tucked in his desk drawer, inhale, relax, and resolve to end this weekend properly, as the happy parent of a sweet toddler, rather than a high-volume harpy who's one bath-toy-projectile away from Googling "safe-harbor locations for kids three and up."

It works.

As I unwind, he responds in kind. I become more patient; he becomes more agreeable. We go to the show, which is teeming with other parents and kids on the continuum between utter bliss and abject frustration. He offers me some Goldfish. I run my fingers through his fine, damp hair and smile at the other parents and babies around me, feeling my heart expand with love and gratitude. It happens a lot, this feeling, but sometimes, just occasionally, I need some chemical help getting there.

In a perfect world, I know, the part about needing some chemical help wouldn't be true. I'd be giving and long-fused and completely present with my child 24/7. But that's not the case. I'm perpetually anxious, often irrationally worried, and my mind is prone to racing for hours like a gerbil on a metal wheel. And three-year-olds are—not to put too fine a point on it—jerks. I mean, not all the time. But frequently. And loudly, for sure.

The fact that I know my son is not going to be that way forever makes it easy to justify an herbal coping strategy every now and again. I don't smoke in front of or anywhere near my child. I almost never drive high (this show was a notable exception). I don't even cook after smoking. What I do is smile more, stress less, and slow the hell down.

I close *The New York Times*, turn off my cell phone, and sit on the floor to do a fourth or fifth puzzle or matching game with my son. I find myself getting lost in the books I read to him, notice things I wouldn't in my usual state, have delightful conversations about what bears dream about or why the stars turn on at night.

But do I feel guilty? After all, mothers are not supposed to need help coping with the very normal business of raising a child. If it's hard, it's hard—we knew that when we signed up. We're definitely not supposed to use illicit substances to mitigate those tough times.

And yet, in the past decade, there's been a profitable trade in painting the modern mother as one who blithely flips the bird at such self-sacrificing notions. Consider the collection of humorous mommy-lit books with titles like *Sippy Cups Are Not for Chardonnay*, *The Three-Martini Playdate*, and *Naptime Is the New Happy Hour*, as well as tongue-in-cheek board books like *Baby, Mix Me a Drink*. Exhausted parents who need a stiff cocktail or two to deal with the baby grind are the stuff of gentle comedy. And where the housewife of the 1960s went stealthily "running for the shelter of her Mother's Little Helper," today that little helper is chilling right there in the refrigerator next to the pureed carrots.

It's hard to imagine a day when *The Three-Puff Playdate* will share shelf space with the books above. Pot is illegal in most states, for one thing, and despite all the solid arguments about why it shouldn't be, that's unlikely to change anytime soon. When I do feel guilty about my occasional tokes, it's mainly because, as a solidly middle-class, educated, white mother living in a city with liberal leaf laws, I have the luxury of even writing an essay that rationalizes the habit.

And I have the further luxury of having only positive associations with parental pot use.

When I was a kid, I remember my father calling me into the family room, where he sat in a nubby red bucket chair, listening to a comedy album on the stereo. "Listen to this one," he urged, as two guys with goofy voices acted out a frustrating comedy of errors.

"It's Dave, man. Open up, I think the cops saw me come in here."

"Dave's not here."

"No man, *I'm* Dave, man. Open up, I got the stuff."

"Dave's not here . . ."

I didn't know that the guys on the record were Cheech & Chong, didn't know that pretty much the entire album was about marijuana, and definitely didn't know that my dad was stoned. All I knew was that he was having fun, laughing a lot, and inviting me to take part in his delight.

My father died when I was thirteen. When I understood, years later and via my older siblings, that smoking pot was one of his small pleasures in life, I suppose it could have occurred to me to second-guess the fun times we had together, chalking them up not to my dad loving my company but simply to a drug-heightened affability that extended to almost anything. (It definitely explained why he was always so excited to go to Burger King on Sunday afternoons.) Instead, it made me feel relieved. Already struggling with a type-A perfectionism that I'd inherited from him, and regularly sidelined by panic attacks and depression, it was a weird comfort to find out that my brilliant, hardworking, successful father needed a toke or two to slow down and just be.

I don't expect to still be smoking when my son hits his own age of experimentation; the last thing I want is to hear an echo of those '80s-era "I learned it from *you*, Mom!" public service announcements. But I hope he'll understand that my secret smokes weren't an attempt to get away from him; that, rather, they were meant to rein in my own churning mind so I could snuggle up and share the world from a vantage point more like his. And yes, so I could have the patience for just one more puzzle, one more tantrum, and a few hundred more questions.

THE END OF CUTE /
SHARON LERNER

a FEW MONTHS BACK, a fellow mother on the playground told me that researchers had just declared that age four-and-a-half was the definitive peak of cuteness in children. The woman delivered this nugget, which horrified and terrified me, as a simple statement of fact. She had read it in a newspaper, I think, and mentioned the finding casually in between sips of decaf and bits of less consequential playground news items. You know: I hear the principal may be retiring next year. The new second grade teacher apparently runs the classroom like a little economy. Oh, and by the way: Your kids will never be this cute again!

I never did look for the study that yielded this finding, though I can imagine how some scientist might have paraded a series of children of various ages in front of adult viewers and measured their prolactin levels or the number of times they said "awww." I picture the adult subjects behind a one-way mirror, with probes affixed to their heads, or perhaps their nipples, as the series of kids appear in front of them. And I have no problem envisioning how, at two and three, the little squishy dumpling people with big eyes, chubby hands and tiny vocabularies elicit far more appreciative sighs and hormone gushes than the stretched out, more self-conscious older ones.

I believe the news she delivered to be true, based on my utterly non-scientific observation that humans have a tendency to melt over puppies, kittens, and baby anythings, and get wiggy around old people. It's not news that adult people aren't particularly cute. The advance is that scientists are finally trying to map and explore this uncharted human territory in between the poles, getting specific about when exactly the enchantment ends and the revulsion begins.

I also viscerally understood what this woman was saying, because as she was delivering the news about the apex of cute, my own kids were teetering on this delicate peak. Actually, they had already tipped over it. Already, there were many occasions when I found them not just uncute, but deeply disgusting. Yes, my own children. My younger son was just then a few weeks past the critical four-and-a-half mark, and my older one was two years ahead of him. Scientifically speaking, their cutest days were behind them.

It seems somehow cruel to distill the appeal of having kids to its short-lived essence. It feels shameful to acknowledge the bald dynamics of the parent-child trade off. But, if we're truthful, we may as well admit to the economics of the parenthood business. We adults get cuddles; dewy, adoring looks; and warm hands to hold—love, if you will—in exchange for providing the care necessary for our little ones to have a chance to survive into adulthood, at which point they may come at this whole bargain from the other side. Those of us who actually plan to have our kids enter into this arrangement willingly and selfishly—if not terribly consciously. Before taking the plunge ourselves, we watch our friends and relatives with their own children, and somehow it seems like a good deal.

From an evolutionary standpoint, you can see why we humans would have developed a combination of chemistry and wiring that draws us to the soft skin, innocent chub, and fine curls of little ones. We need something to get us through the middle-of-the-night risings, tantrums, and diaper changes. So if their shit smells terrible, their plump little folds of their thighs are so enticing, it doesn't really matter! And the way they mispronounce "machine," as in, "There's a bunny-destroying chamine under my bed!" makes you almost forgive the fact that they're saying this adorable thing at three in the morning.

The problem is, if their charms dissipate, the challenges and annoyances children pose clearly do not. This part I know, among other ways, from having posed such challenges and annoyances to my own parents. Lying, drugs, mischief—I did it all when I was younger. What's more: I committed the worst of it, I now realize with horror, long after my baby fat was gone and my formerly soft face had broken out in blackheads and other nasty blemishes.

Thankfully, my parents held off on killing me. But putting a precise number on the end of cute leads me to wonder whether I will be able to pass on the evolutionary favor my parents bestowed upon me. More to the immediate point, I worry that my next few years will be spent in a gradual downward slide toward the unpleasant prospect of dealing with progressively less cute boys doing even less cute things. Had these past few years, filled with cuddly bedtime stories and games of "egg," in which I sat on my boys' balled up bodies waiting for them to "hatch," been as good as it was going to get? Ever?

And then there's the disturbing truth—my disturbing truth—that, even while at their theoretically cutest, my kids have always also been the opposite of cute: i.e., gross. At the pudgiest and most magical stage of his toddlerhood, when even the sourest of passersby could be caught flashing silly grins at him, one of my sons pooped in his room. This, of course, is pretty standard fare for little kids. What made this particular incident of defecation noteworthy is that we knew nothing of it at the time. To his credit, my little one quickly disposed of it.

To his discredit—or at least our misfortune—he put it in his radiator. Secretly. We only discovered the hidden stash much later, when a foul odor prompted a sniff search that ultimately led his father and me to two desiccated turds perched on the heating coil.

Meanwhile, pretty much every meal consumed during the peak cute years has contained an element of horror. Yes, sure, there is a primal joy to be had in feeding your offspring, knowing that each bite gets them that much bigger and stronger; that with each meal, I am not just providing sustenance but continuing a process that has enabled an age-old series of organisms to evolve into these particular small creatures sitting at my table. But I never actually think such thoughts during our dinners, so focused am I on their little sauce-smeared hands as they caress their noodles; the thread of regurgitated cheese sauce that one of them has backwashed into my water glass; or the piece of scrambled egg that clings almost magically to one of their curls. Ew.

If the cuteness (which clearly offsets the disgust in some complex way yet to be studied) continues to dissipate, I fear I'll have nothing to get me through dinner. Already, my six-year-old has shed much of his magical early childhood softness. Being short, like me, he can look younger than he is. But when you pick him up and he squeezes you between his vise-like thighs, you know. It takes years to develop the ropey muscularity he has. His little brother never seemed to have much baby fat. He didn't have those bracelet-like folds of skin that form around some infants' wrists or the hefty thighs that beg to be squeezed. Now, the tiny bit of chub remaining around his belly button seems to be getting smaller by the day. And most times when I try to gather it in my hand for a quick squish, he brushes me off with a mildly annoyed "Mom!" that might as well spring from the mouth of a teenager.

Perhaps it was my instinctive knowledge that the end of cute was upon us that sparked my nightly ritual of watching my kids sleep. Since the littler one turned four, I've been stopping into their rooms at night before I head to mine, crouching by their beds where I can still smell the cuteness in their breath. These visits seem to erase whatever awfulness might have transpired during the day. With their stuffed animals held tight, their eyes closed, and their chests gently heaving, my kids are still little and cute at night.

I begin to conjure these nighttime forays while I'm still standing on the playground. By now, the mother who delivered the bomb has left, unaware that she has launched a panic about the dwindling cuteness of my children. And I'm onto devising solutions. Perhaps it'll be enough to continue my nighttime visits well into adolescence. If my boys will be acne-covered and hostile during the day, maybe at night they'll retain some of their current sweetness, even as they snore away in their dirty-sock-scented rooms. Adolescent night visits could function sort of like dialysis: spending a certain amount of time inhaling their sleepy breath could provide me the strength to handle whatever icky affronts they bring during the day.

I'm enjoying the thought of myself stealing into the bedrooms of my teenagers, drinking their breath like medicine, when my older son suddenly body slams me on the playground. He tries hard not to cry, so I know whatever has driven him to smoosh his face into my jacket must be pretty serious. But as usual, he offers no details, keeping his head silently pressed into me as the tears subside. It's a childlike pose if there ever was one—crying and clutching your mother for comfort. But, as I look down on him, I realize he doesn't look cute—or, rather, he doesn't just look cute.

Spurred, no doubt, by my recent brush with the research, I try to affect a scientific eye as I scrutinize this strange creature attached to me. I see the dark, crescent-moon of playground dirt under each of his nails; the way his wiry curls, already so much more like an adult's than a baby's, grow way lower down on his forehead than where most people's hairlines begin; the snot that's smeared across his right cheek—and, now, yes, on my jacket, too. And it occurs to me that already there is already so much that is not cute about him—or at least "cute" in the sense that it would register as such in a research study.

As I'm waiting for him to pull back away from me and rejoin the kickball game, I'm struck by the familiar guilt of being grossed out by my own kid. The truth is, as far back as infancy, when they should have been squarely in the cute zone, my kids have always been a little gross. Of course, all kids are a little gross—all people are a little gross. What's risky to admit, perhaps, is that I've always noticed this grossness in my own kids, and I've often been repelled by it. Their cuteness hasn't always trumped their disgustingness, as seems to be the case for some other parents.

I remember the first time one of my sons vomited. Nothing had prepared me for the force of the stream of hot liquid that spewed forth from that little mouth. For an instant, I stood transfixed by the bizarre sight of my tiny baby turned vomit fountain. But instinct soon kicked in—though not, sadly, the maternal kind. As the arc of vomit splashed onto my arm, I almost struck my son's head against our kitchen counter, so quickly did I move him away from me.

I have rehashed that moment often—always feeling shame that my impulse was to move my child away from—rather than toward me. (Contrast that with the mother in our baby group who showed up with photos of the diarrhea that her infant had squirted across the room and onto the books on her shelf. Her face lit up with unmistakable pride as she scrolled through numerous shots of shit-strewn books.)

I've asked myself what sort of person feels revulsion for her own young, and I never quite come up with a satisfying answer. Yet standing with my arms around my short, muscly son with dirty nails and wiry hair, it occurs to me that I am the sort of mother who feels revulsion, occasionally, for her young children, just as I am also the sort of mother who looks forward to drinking her boys' night breath for years to come.

The thought puts me at ease with the inevitable end of cute, or at least the end of the universally recognizable kind of cute. It may be at four, or five, at six, or at twenty, but whenever it is, by the time the strange pull of cuteness wears off, it doesn't matter. We don't love kids because they're cute. It just helps us get stuck together. And we don't love them any less because they're sometimes revolting. It is a fact of childhood—of life—that we accept with varying amounts of grace.

As my son finally, wordlessly releases me and runs off to rejoin his friends, I feel sure that, no matter what befalls his now silky skin or how bad his armpits wind up smelling, I'm going to want to make him feel better, whatever it is that upsets him so.

THE MACARONI AND CHEESE DILEMMA /
LIZ HENRY

WHEN I TURNED THIRTY, the urge to have a baby seemed like a sudden-onset epidemic among the women around me. They yearned—even begged—to become pregnant. If they weren't putting pressure on their existing partners to procreate, they were trawling for potential poppas—preferably someone with the main criteria of availability. These were women who had once been girls. Girls who were softball teammates and concert-going, chain-smoking good times. Some of them had drifted through jobs without purpose, while others had well-defined education and career goals they were trying to reach. But once thirty hit, they were all on the same life course: motherhood.

I, on the other hand, had been there, done that, and bought the

T-shirt—a good decade before them. The last thing I wanted was a second child. Sure, hand me a baby and I will coo adoringly and pinch cheeks and change diapers. And I will do it lovingly, because I really do enjoy babies. But I enjoy babies most when they are not mine and I do not have to pay for them or find a place to live within a school district that's not a demilitarized zone, or find the elusive "balance" between my goals and what's best for a new, precious bundle.

At this moment, I feel compelled to tell you that I love my daughter. She is hilarious and I hope that one day all of her TV-watching amounts to her winning an Oscar, or at least a stint on *Saturday Night Live*. But what if I didn't feel compelled to tell you that I loved her and that I was a good mother, and instead simply stated that I had no desire to become a mother again? Would it mean I loved her any less? Or that I was somehow less of a mother for not wanting a second child?

Ten years ago I was ambivalent about becoming a mother. Quite frankly, I never thought about it. Hell, I was barely an adult. Sure, I had goals, but they were abstract things like "go to college" and "become a writer." These were lofty ambitions in my family since no one had attended or graduated from college. In my mom's case, it was circumstance: a few months before her high school graduation, she found herself unexpectedly pregnant with my sister. She would ultimately receive a diploma and the scorn of her Catholic high school, but that's it. And to save face, she'd opt for a quick wedding in my grandparents' backyard. In a way, my mother's legacy would become mine: a year into college I would find myself pregnant, and like her I would choose to give birth. But I would make my own path, forging ahead with sleepless nights spent writing papers while my infant daughter swayed back and forth in a motorized swing, and my twenty-first birthday came and went without booze.

And just like that, my carefree twenties left me before they even began. I sucked it up and rarely slept. I stuck my daughter in front of the TV while reading articles about how I should never do such a thing. I studied, read, and wrote through trips to the Jersey Shore as my partner and my daughter went to the beach. I signed up for WIC, Food Stamps, and Medicaid so I could remain an insured college student and mother who survived on $12,000 a year. I broke down in tears in a Women's Studies class, hyperventilating that I was crumbling under the pressure of motherhood.

This was all in the first three years.

I was an epic mess. Fuck, I am still a mess, but back then I was breaking down in front of my own doctor during a physical because I felt so guilty about feeding my daughter Kraft Macaroni and Cheese, which I knew was over-processed crap meant for the apocalypse instead of a run-of-the-mill Wednesday night dinner. I was convinced that the navy blue box and its envelope of cheese sand would stunt my daughter's potential, and that despite my time constraints, I should be cooking something nutritious and probably organic instead. As I sat on the edge of the exam table and melted down like a hunk of butter in a pot of starchy macaroni—my doctor looked at me and said, "Let her have the mac and cheese." She said it with such ease that I immediately knew I was putting too much pressure on myself. That it was just a tad insane of me to think that I should be milking a cow, pressing the noodles, and aging the cheese myself in order to feel like I was a good mother.

And it wasn't just over-processed food that distressed me during those first few years. When I complained to my mother that all of my peers were living adventurous, carefree, creative lives that seemed exotic by comparison, she'd say, "It's frustrating, I know, you're watching all of your friends come and go as they please, but when they settle down to have their babies, you'll be revving and they'll be settling. You're doing it in reverse, but it all equalizes in the end."

Oh, how I clung to those two sentences like they were chiseled in stone and lifted on high from the Mountain of Truer Words Have Never Been Spoken. Her words became my plan, and I was sticking to it. I would cook this meal here, and volunteer my time there, and continue my sleepless nights, all for love and the greater good in the hopes that eventually there would come a time when I got to be me again. When I could sit without interruption, write *and* sleep, earn without daycare and leave without guilt.

And eventually, it began to happen.

After ten years, my partner and I were still together, our little triangle-shaped family unit was solid, and I was no longer losing my shit over noodles. I had graduated college years before and was beginning to give writing the real shot it deserved. And then, in a case of bitter irony, I found myself pregnant again, alongside all my thirty-something friends. But unlike them, I wasn't interested in riding this wave. From the moment I thought I was pregnant, to the time I confirmed it with two lines (and then a few more thrown in for good measure), I knew this pregnancy was wrong. It even felt wrong in the pit of my stomach. I couldn't move from my bed, I couldn't leave the shower without drying myself in despair. This pregnancy was not what I wanted. How could I start all over again? How could I take from the one that I had for another that was yet to be?

It was time to decide.

I knew what abortion entailed, I had witnessed it firsthand. Before I graduated college, I had interned at Planned Parenthood as a grant writer. On Friday mornings, I would drop my daughter off with her babysitter, and then hold the hands of women who opted to have an abortion rather than carry their pregnancies to term. While interning, I saw the faces of young and middle-aged, married and single, poor and with means. I heard stories of sadness and relief. I witnessed women recover and leave to the embrace of their friends or partners, mothers or fathers. Everyone had someone to support them, even if that support was my hand.

I knew that one in three women would have an abortion before their child-bearing years were over, and that most of them already had children at home. For me, abortion was not something I talked about in hushed whispers, but a safe medical procedure I witnessed every Friday for almost a year.

Having another child would have altered my life in much the same way it changes every mother's, but this time I was not prepared to make that sacrifice. Sadness would have engulfed my very being and followed me around like a shadow. There would be no time for getting ahead or quieting the ambitions that lay dormant, waiting for the right season to flourish. In purely selfish terms, I was not prepared for months of overwhelming sickness or pushing another bundle through the Ring of Fire. (Johnny Cash, by the way, was clearly singing about his wife giving birth. And no one can convince me otherwise.)

My decision was made.

As I made my way to the clinic on the appointed day, I was not weighted by a heavy heart or any regret. This was simply an appointment to end an unwanted pregnancy. I knew the steps I would need to take when I arrived, and had already viewed the state-mandated video informing me that, by law, the father was compelled to provide me with child support. And just in case I was wondering, having an abortion could lead to death. Just like, you know, child birth could (which they didn't mention).

My name was called, my finger was pricked, my weight was logged, and then my clothes were off. I was on the table, legs spread and cervix numbed before I felt the pain. It was longer than I expected; a take-your-breath-away, grab-onto-something, anything-because-this-is-unbearable pain. And right before I thought I was about to scream, it was over.

I was no longer pregnant.

I made my way to the recovery room, where a nurse gently placed a heating pad on my abdomen, poured ginger ale into a clear plastic cup, and divided graham crackers for my consumption. I drank and munched as more women came and went, some with tears, and others, like me, who just wanted to go home and get on with their lives.

I had an abortion, and the world didn't end. In fact, it saved the life

I have: breakdowns over macaroni and cheese, my child overdosing on TV, writing into the wee hours of the night, and not to be forgotten, my love for other people's children. I hedged my bets on the family I already had instead of growing into the one I didn't want.

My mother was right: It all equalizes in the end.

MAKING TIME FOR LUST / **ERIKA LUST**

“**W**HO SHOULD I MAKE IT OUT TO?”
I smiled up at the middle-aged couple, my pen paused above the DVD of my latest film.

"Alex . . ."

To Alex, I begin.

". . . my son."

I stop and look up again, this time with surprise. The mother shrugs. "He's sixteen, he watches porn anyway. I'd rather have him watching yours."

My partner, Pablo, and I were in Girona, Spain, for an art-house screening of *Cabaret Desire,* an indie adult film I'd written and directed the previous year. In my line of work, there is always this amazing interplay of sex and parenthood: No matter how much people want to keep the two separated, they're impossibly entwined. We spent an amazing weekend there in Girona—full of parties, interviews and tours—which felt like a vacation, even though it was only an hour up the highway from our home in Barcelona.

Just five years ago, this little taste of paradise would not have been possible. Our eldest daughter, Lara, was born in 2007, and there was a long period where I was very protective and anxious about my new role. When she was around five months old, Pablo suggested we have a weekend away all to ourselves, much like the one I just described in Girona. Even though I knew he wanted to reconnect with me (and maybe get a real night's sleep), I balked at the idea and couldn't get over the thought of physical separation from my daughter. In the end, Pablo and his winning common sense got the better of me, and we left Lara with his sister for the weekend.

I cringe when I think of how I spent that whole first night bawling into a crisp hotel pillow over the fact that my little girl was a ten-minute taxi ride away from us. But at the time, she might as well have been on the moon. The second night, I relaxed enough over a glass of *Rioja* and an endless Spanish dinner to realize that I was looking at my partner for the first time in five months—looking at him and actually seeing the man I dated and fell in love with, full of excitement, smiles and sarcastic humor. When had he become this ghost in my peripheral vision, the extension of myself as a co-parent that I'd been living with for months? And what, for that matter, had I become to him in that time? In the end, that didn't really matter, because as we sat flirting, joking, and giving playful squeezes under the table, I settled into my old self again and so did Pablo.

I remember this weekend so clearly, because it was when I discovered how important it was to remove the motherhood mantle for a while: not only for my well being, but also for that of my relationship. This is why Pablo and I made a promise to one another: one date a week, one weekend a month, and one week per year with no kids, just us. I can't say we follow this to a tee, but we try, and that's what matters. This is the same reason that I love going to work so much. By the time I've gotten our daughters (now aged two and five) up, bathed, fed, clothed, and ready for school, I feel like I've negotiated and mitigated more than the average lawyer. I love arriving to the office, seeing ERIKA LUST printed on the door, sitting down at my desk, and feeling a restorative sense of control and calm that I get from being my own boss.

What's funny about my line of work is that people just assume that I have a leg-up, so to speak, when it comes to keeping the relationship alive in the bedroom. To be honest, I feel I have some advantage, in that working in the adult industry really reinforces the importance of sex in maintaining intimacy. On the other hand, that gem of wisdom only made me feel guilty when sex was the furthest thing from my mind. And that is something that no mother can escape. It's only too easy to become an asexual parent when you factor in the lack of sleep, stress, and inherently unsexy tasks that face those who are rearing a child: diaper explosions, food riots, temper tantrums, and unstoppable crying jags —at the end of one of those days, I am in absolutely no physical or psychological state to feel sexy or want sex. On top of it, it seems deeply unfair that, under the same circumstances, Pablo would have no qualms about hopping in to the sack.

Be that as it may, I have to find the time to have, and indeed want to have, sex just like any other parent. And trust me, it's hard. We have two small girls and run our own business: in fact, often times our dates have to be penciled-in like business meetings. It's not like I shoot explicit films all day and then want to rip my clothes off the minute the apartment door closes. Rather, on Friday night, even if I'm grumbling about how much I just want to curl up on the couch, I head to the wardrobe and exchange my sneakers for some sleek boots, my hoodie for a leather jacket. I've stopped thinking about the couch by the time I'm curling my hair and applying lipstick in the bathroom, reminiscing instead about getting ready for a college party. And by the time I slide into a booth next to Pablo, gourmet cocktail in hand, I feel absolutely sultry.

In this way, being a mother is hugely inspiring for me. By

challenging my own sexuality, motherhood forces me to realize that sometimes getting to the bedroom isn't as natural, fun, or easy as what is done in the bedroom itself. And this is something I'm trying more and more to infuse in my films: one example being an installment called, "Married with Children," where a very seemingly normal couple by day lose themselves in a world of S&M by night. I want to impart to my viewers, and parents especially, that sex, lust, and passion are absolutely worth having in your life, even if it is incredibly difficult to manifest at times. I hope not only to inspire others in this sense, but to continue to be inspired by others . . . like Alex's parents at the Girona screening, who were not only so accepting of his sexuality, but also of their own. In this way, I hope we can keep inspiring each other to break down the divide between sex and parenting.

TO BE REAL /
CANDACE WALSH

FRESHMAN YEAR OF COLLEGE, I spent a Saturday afternoon in my dorm room, sitting in a big black easy chair my roommate and I had thrifted. My friends were hanging out on the lawn, catching late fall rays, on a rare balmy day in Buffalo, listening to music, laughing. I was scribbling furiously in my journal.

"When I become a mother," I wrote, "I will do everything in my power to give my children a normal, stable life. I won't marry the wrong man like my mother did. I will marry someone who will be a wonderful father. My kids will have nice clothes and shoes, and will never worry about the electric being shut off. We'll drive a reliable car, nothing fancy, just not an old clunker. Otherwise, I shouldn't have children. It's just not responsible."

Why wasn't I outside enjoying myself? Why was I writing down this declaration at the tender age of seventeen? I certainly wasn't going to have kids for at least five to ten years. But something inside me demanded that I be accountable long before I became a parent.

The distance I had from home that first semester away had given me some room to see all that I did not want to pass on to the next generation. By the time I left my Long Island home to go to college in Buffalo, I'd moved over ten times. No, we weren't a military family. We were just a mess. Alcoholism, nervous breakdowns, irresponsible spending, religious extremism, then divorce, and my own near death at the hands of my new stepfather, who tried to strangle me one day. After that, he wasn't thrown out of the house, I was. My mother said that she was afraid that she'd lose custody of the rest of her kids, and she didn't think she could survive financially without him.

I sat in that black chair and scribbled furiously because I knew I had no model for a happy, stable life. I had to build it from the ground up.

I did eventually leave the chair, the room. College had its way with me. Within that bubble, I realized that I had a tendency to fall for women in more profound ways than I did for men. My relationships with guys always seemed to boil down to the same power struggle: I focused on fickle free spirits and tried to turn them into doting house cats. It was as if I thought taming them would change all of masculinity, would solve my earliest disjunction, the one with my father and later with my stepfather. The passion to remake my history fueled these pursuits more than anything else. It was so strong that it felt like love. But I never did tame a single one of those guys, or earn lasting devotion. By the time I left school, I wasn't clear on all of this, but I was open to dating women.

But in the post-collegiate years of the mid-nineties, my aversion to being different grew with every new job and social circle I encountered. German bank in New York City's financial district? Not gay-friendly. Fashion magazines? Gay-friendly . . . but only for gay men. My father grew warmer toward me as I encountered modest success as a young writer. Did I want to lose that precious gain for an abstract relationship with some unknown woman? And how would all that affect my desire for my own family to be steeped in normal? My life felt both as fragile and as stable as a spider web, as long as I didn't shake it up.

I fell for another half dozen noncommittal, unreliable men. I told myself I liked a challenge, but I really think I liked my space, even if that space was oppressively filled with yearning for companionship.

Sticking to my guns, when I was twenty-six, I broke up with the charismatic, dashing man who made it clear he wasn't husband material, both verbally and by tomcatting around at every opportunity. I had to make space for my true other half—someone who was responsible, serious, smart, and ambitious. No matter what, he had to be a good dad. That was the first criterion. Everything else was secondary.

A few months later, I met someone who was eminently promising. He was clean-cut, studious, intelligent, well-spoken. He was a hard worker and extremely tidy. He, too, had had a tumultuous upbringing, and we both were dead-set on breaking those patterns and making stable lives for ourselves. We fell in love.

Less than a year later, we were married. Another year after that, we were parents, and moved to New Mexico. Unfortunately, we were still living in reaction to our childhoods—making choices based on what we didn't want, instead of teasing out what we did.

Then we had another child. Their needs were abundantly met, and I drove a reliable car. Their father was respectable, and I passed for the same. I took my daughter and son to the children's museum and the park, they went to the safe choice preschool, and always brought meticulously wrapped presents to birthday parties.

But as the years went by, under the surface I was drenched in misery, and my husband was too. Although our life together was stable, we came to realize that there was a lot more to a satisfying life than that. I felt like a fraud. Sitting through birthday parties felt like getting dental work. I could barely wait to get home whenever we went out. I was withdrawn, distracted, craved inertia. There was a long time when I just thought that I was a depressed loser. But then I began to sense that I could be a livelier, happier person if my life was different. "Your children are going to be pretty confused about love if they grow up with parents who pretend to care about each other but don't really feel it," a friend told me.

The misery was like gasoline, and one errant spark would blow our life to kingdom come.

When it did, I found myself in the reliable car, my children in the back seat, driving their innocent, unknowing little selves to their new house. Mommy's house, in contrast to Daddy's house, as these were now separate. There were so many tears, ones I'd always thought I could prevent by making different choices than my parents had. First I made my children, in my body, then I made them sad with my decision. Whenever your kids feel pain, you want to make it all better. I yearned to be able to neatly fix their toppled worlds. But a quick fix would only seal my fate—and theirs, to a subtler extent.

I couldn't give my children the rock-solid, affluent, dream childhood I'd always intended. We no longer live in that particular beautiful house on the hill with two new cars. They aren't still taking French, dance, art lessons, and they've moved a handful of times as my ex-husband and I have settled into our new lives and homes. I don't buy them clothes by the bagful during trips to New York or Paris. My daughter has cello lessons, my son plays soccer, and they go to summer camp at the local rec center. The children move between our two households every other week. However, those two households are stable, run by parents who are not perfect, but definitely cheerful and content. I did choose correctly in that regard. The kids have a devoted, present, loving father, and a happy, energetic mother.

This wasn't the plan I drew up in that black chair. Especially given that after my marriage ended, I switched teams. I clicked "Woman seeking Women" on the Match.com profile box. When the kids were with their dad, I went, quavering with fear, to women's dances and events. I had reason to believe that having a gay mom wouldn't make the kids' lives easier, but I also knew that continuing to toe the heteronormative line would plunge me back into depression and dishonesty—and that would affect them negatively every day.

I had always told the kids that they could marry whoever they wanted—boy, girl—whoever they loved, hoping that by the time they were old enough to do so, marriage equality would be in place. So when I did tell them that I was dating a woman, they didn't think it was abnormal. When I introduced them to Laura after three months of dating, they loved her on sight. My ex was supportive of my shift, so they didn't hear anything negative from him.

It was when they talked enthusiastically at school about having three moms—me, Laura, and their father's girlfriend—that they started to get disturbing reactions. "Your mom goes out with a woman? That's weird/gross/wrong!" said my daughter's private school peers. Every few months, I'd have to call the teacher, telling him that it needed to be addressed. "Can't you just make an announcement about tolerance and difference, so that we don't have to go through this with each kid?" I asked, but that didn't happen. He did talk to the students, and sometimes, the parents. It was awkward. I hugged my daughter, told her that I was sorry that she had to deal with these encounters because of our family structure. And that I was sorry that she had to put up with people saying unpleasant things about me.

"There's nothing wrong with you and Laura!" she said. "You love each other, and we love you both."

I didn't want to press them into activist roles, but they were indignant of their own accord when a local burger chain donated $100,000 to defeat marriage equality in California. "We're not eating there any more," my son declared.

When we put the kids in our local public school, my daughter had to encounter a whole new group of responses. Several kids told her that if she had a gay mom, she would surely be gay too. The ignorance that she has to wade through, attempt to dispel, just to define herself, is daunting, and it's nothing I would have chosen for her. My son is at the age where having three moms is the coolest thing ever. I hope it stays that way. And their school teachers, counselor, and principal were amazingly responsive the first time a kid crossed the line; far more responsive than the private school had been.

We've been fortunate enough to be in a position to make choices that have decreased potential friction—we settled in a liberal, open-minded neighborhood, and before I got a more demanding job, I made a special point of volunteering at school to be visible as just another mom in khaki trousers and a cozy cardigan (I definitely dressed thoughtfully those days).

When New York legalized same-sex marriage in 2011, I called my daughter at her friend's house—she was at a sleepover—to tell her the news. She and I jumped up and down on opposite sides of the phone line, screaming, "Yay!" I could hear her friend cheering, too. My son danced around the living room with Laura. We got married four months later, in my home state, with select friends and family present. It was joyous. And it still is, every day, despite the frustrations common to daily life.

I sometimes sense the reproach of the girl in the black chair. But I let it float on by. My children have a happy mother. The love that flows so freely in our household soothes them like a constant lullaby. And the concept of living one's truth is as familiar to my children as I am.

LUCKY AMERICAN GIRL /
K. J. DELL'ANTONIA

tHIS IS A SMALL PART OF THE STORY of a year in my life when I really, really sucked. Which would be fine—who hasn't been their worst possible self for a year or two, or ten—except that I'd just convinced China that I could be the best possible mother to a three-year-old who allegedly needed just that, and neither China, nor that three-year-old, nor I, had expected me to suck at the job.

Before I embarked on my extended voyage of sucking, there was nothing I wanted more in the world than to adopt a daughter. A little girl to be a younger sister for my Lily, nearly five at the time. Another girl to even the scales against Wyatt, just three, and Sam, who would turn eight on the exact day that our newest child was delivered (unceremoniously, and amidst screams of rage and the infuriated beating of her fists) into our lives. Except for the fury, Wan was everything I'd asked for: spirited and open-hearted, nearly four, and well able to hold her own in our personal family carnival.

In truth, after that ignominious beginning, Wan—who already had, in her mind, a perfectly good family and no real interest in becoming part of ours—would handle the pancake flip of her entire identity with all of the grace you could reasonably expect from a three-year-old.

I would not.

I would not handle becoming Wan's mother with any grace at all, whatsoever—not sufficient grace for a thirty-nine-year-old writer, former prosecutor, and mother of three. Not even sufficient grace had I been three myself.

We heard Wan before we saw her. We'd hoped to meet her at her foster home. Instead, we were instructed to come to a conference room at the top floor of our hotel. As the last two floors ticked away on the lighted list over our heads, her distant staccato shrieks grew louder, reaching top volume as the elevator doors opened.

In a bland room of coffee tables, long drapes, and beige sofas, Wan sat—or rather, Wan lay—half on the floor, half propped rigid against one of the sofas, kicking her feet frantically and screaming. Frantic, horrible, repeated screams, barely decipherable. "I … WANT … GO … HOME!" On either side of her knelt two young Chinese women, equally frantic but far less terrified, saying soothing things that no one could hear, and Wan, even had she heard, could not understand. Wan spent her first years in a foster home run by Americans; she spoke English, not Mandarin.

With barely a glance at the male official standing, helpless, off to one side, I did the only thing I would do right all week. There was no doubt that this was our Wan. We had Skyped with her as she sat in her foster mother's lap, sung to her on a DVD she'd watched again and again, sent her, in fact, the shoes she was wearing. I ran to her and knelt next to her, between the coffee table and the sofa, putting my arms around her fierce stance. I whispered in her ear as she paused, startled.

"It's us," I said, too softly for anyone else to hear. "Mama said we would come. Baba said we would come for you. It's okay to go with us. It's okay. We'll take care of you."

And the whole room, including me, froze as Wan stopped screaming and subsided into gulps and soft sobs in my arms.

China's original plan had been for us to spend two days with Wan, then return with her to finalize our paperwork. What we'd been given earlier in the day was merely temporary custody. This was a system created to give adoptive parents time to assure themselves that they really wanted the child, or to discover any hidden medical issues, but it had long since become (except in a few sad cases) a formality. Because Wan's home province had a public holiday the next day, its officials had decided to bypass the time requirement. We should, we'd been told, return upstairs with Wan that afternoon to sign the rest of the papers necessary to make Wan our daughter, at least as far as China was concerned.

But first, we had time to kill, and with four kids packed into a hotel room, that time was already dragging. I didn't expect the beginning of a new phase in all of our lives to be fraught with sheer banality. Wan was exhausted. We found out later from the officials who'd brought her to us that they'd torn a screaming Wan from the arms of someone from her foster home. The women we'd met upstairs told our guide that she had kicked, screamed, and bitten the whole way to the hotel, except for a brief interval when they plied her with a lollipop. From Wan herself, almost a year later, we discovered that it had been a "very small lollipop."

Our original three kids had long since accepted the limitations of hotel life. Wan had not. Under the fascinated gaze of her new siblings, she roamed the room with the safety scissors and crayons we had given her in hand, unable to sit down to anything, and not familiar enough with her new brothers or sister to understand how to play with them. Before long, she'd abandoned the crayons and had cut every piece of paper she could get her hands on into tiny shreds. As long as I was watching her, she was fine. If I turned my attention away, she left the paper I'd given her and began to prowl for other cutting opportunities until I focused on her again. I hovered, rescuing sofa cushions, the rug, the curtains. Sam and Lily tried to distract Wan. Wyatt followed her until she screamed.

I felt compelled to do something meaningful to pull all of this together, but I felt like I was failing. There was my mom, in the armchair in the corner, watching her only child become a mother of four. There was Rob, who'd put up with so much to fulfill this dream of mine, still manfully shuffling papers and kowtowing to Chinese demands—after just half an hour of bonding with his new daughter and her safety scissors, he'd gone with our guide to complete still more paperwork. There were Sam, Lily, and Wyatt. This was their new sister, we'd told them. I was her Mommy, too. They knew me as a Mommy full of love and patience and discipline and familiarity. What could they expect of me now? Was it comforting, or terrifying, to see me try to mother even so small a stranger?

And there was Wan. Wan, moving determinedly through that hotel room like a wind-up toy, unable to stop and unable to rest. How could she bear so much strangeness? I can only think that she couldn't, and that with every snip of the scissors, she was cutting off the risk that she might feel it in full.

After lunch, we set back out for that upstairs conference room. I was afraid that Wan would think we were giving her back to what had clearly been her tormentors.

"You're coming back with us," I whispered to her. "You can stay with me the whole time, and then we will go back downstairs together." Wan didn't respond. She sat rigid on my arms as though I were just anyone, as though I were a chair or a rail, and she didn't look at me, but leaned instead toward the wall of buttons on the elevator.

When we walked into the same room we'd found her in that morning, with the same young women, the same older man, Wan struggled down from my arms. She didn't cry or scream. Instead, she climbed up on the coffee table. There, looking squarely at the face of the Fuzhou official, she stomped first one foot and then the other before she began to jump up and down with a fierce passion.

The young women laughed. The man smiled grimly. "She is not very Chinese," he said.

"No," I agreed as Rob lifted her off the table and put her back on my lap and she immediately squirmed off again to go explore the curtains, "she's not."

It was a sentiment we'd hear again and again, from guides, drivers, and adoption facilitators in first one town, and then another. In Guangzhou, on our final stop in China, the last of our guides gazed at the child who spent the entire trip running from her stroller or screaming for "Ice cream! Ice cream! ICE CREAM!" and said it again, thoughtfully. "She not very Chinese." But this guide also thought Wan was lucky, and even seemed to admire her spirit. "She lucky American girl."

I was the one who did not feel lucky, although I should have. The child we'd brought into our family was clearly no ordinary child, and she was desperately trying to find her place with us. If "not very Chinese" meant "very willing to do whatever she could to get what she wanted," then Wan was indeed not very Chinese, and what Wan wanted was me.

She liked Rob fine. But we have long had a family dynamic of competing for Mommy, and Wan picked up on it immediately. If I was the most valued parent to the ever-grappling Lily and Wyatt, then she would grapple, too. She was not going to settle for second best.

She quickly discovered that "I have to go potty" meant instant alone time with Mommy, and dragged me to bathroom after bathroom. Insisted that I, and only I, push her around China in the stroller. Made me lie with her at night before she went to sleep; begged me for "uppy" at every turn; wanted to wear my hat, take my glasses, hold my bag. She'd set Wyatt up, leaning over him, hanging, poking, hitting him softly until he returned the hit, and then she'd scream for me.

It was just her bad luck that I was watching, because some of the time, Wyatt did hit her. All of that uppy and lappy and mommy-time she was getting? He wanted some of that, too.

Wan didn't just want my attention, she wanted me to do what she wanted me to do: cut her food, feed her, hold her drink, hold her hand, carry her. Reading that list now is like reading the recommendations of an attachment expert. But everything I did for her was something I didn't do for Wyatt or Lily. Every minute talking to her was a minute not listening to Sam's enthusiastic observations about China. And every minute in the bathroom was another smelly, restricted opportunity for this child I barely knew to manage to pee on my shoes. As for Wan, she woke up in the night calling for "Mama," and greeted my arrival with fresh tears.

I thought I was ready to be Wan's parent, but I have rarely been more wrong. There was so much I didn't understand. I had fallen so fully for the "child who needs a family" trope that I hadn't ever considered that my new daughter would be just as grieved and terrified by that idea as Wyatt would be, if someone picked him up and handed him off while I waved good-bye. That's hard to consider even in the abstract. The confused, willful, demanding child in front of me made it—and my part in it—real. She took the illusion I'd cherished, the one where I masterminded the coming together of the big happy family, and shredded it like a hotel notepad.

The evening before we left Guangzhou, Wan staged a mid-sidewalk sit-down strike between the hotel and the restaurant. She would go no further unless I carried her.

I had held her all through dinner, spilling hot bites of soup and chopsticks of spicy pork into my lap, trying to get them around her squirms and into my own mouth. Every time my attention shifted, she'd declared her need to go "potty," and we had gone, coming back to one cold course after another. I was hungry. I was angry. I was tired. I would not pick her up.

I waved Rob on, and with a dubious look, he hoisted Wyatt to his hip and shepherded everyone else away from the scene. Wan wailed. She howled. She sat her butt down on the filthy sidewalk and stuck her legs straight out in front of her. She beat the ground with her fists and heels. I sat on a stoop about ten feet away and I let her.

Guangzhou is the final stop for every single Chinese person immigrating to the United States, and that includes adoptees, so the people of its streets were used to seeing white parents wrestle with unwilling Chinese young. Some stopped. They knelt to help the poor, screaming child, speaking to her in Chinese, which only made her scream more loudly. From my post on the stoop, I stopped the would-be Samaritans with my terrible Mandarin.

"No," I said. "She not Chinese. She bad American girl." Most laughed, and I did my best to smile back, knowing they assumed that Wan had been adopted years before.

Five times I got up and I hissed in her ear. "Mommy will take you back to the hotel as soon as you walk. Get up, walk, and Mommy will take you back to the hotel." I waved a big family of Americans through, one bearing a placid Chinese toddler. I took shallow breaths.

Wan stood up. She stuck her hand out at me. "I walk!

"Come here, then."

She didn't move. "I walk! Hand!"

I thrust out my own hand. "Then come here."

Her mouth hung open, and her face and body stilled. She dropped her hand to her side and waited.

I thrust my hand out again, harder. "Come here." My voice came out cracked and ugly.

Wan walked to me and put her hand in mine.

I'd won. I felt a crazed mixture of triumph and misery. I'd shown her she needed to do what I said. I'd refused to be manipulated. She'd given in. But what kind of mother—*what kind of mother*—refuses to carry a confused, lost, three-year-old just days after her entire world has been destroyed?

We walked the half-block back to find the others eating a final ice cream outside the hotel. Before Wan could demand hers, I picked her up and carried her to the counter. She sat on my arms like you'd sit on a branch. She didn't reach for me. I had to lean her body into mine to keep from dropping her. She took the vanilla cone with both hands and licked it with a hungry rhythm as I balanced her into a seat and looked at Rob over her hair.

He shook his head at me.

I looked to my mother, but her lips were tight. She leaned over to wipe Wyatt's face with a napkin, refusing to meet my eye.

"She just can't do that," I said weakly.

Rob shrugged. "We have to go pack."

The bad American girl and her bad American mother were going home.

MY ONLINE LIFE AS A (NOT SO) LESBIAN MAMA /
CHRISTINA SOLETTI

I ALWAYS WANTED TO BE A MAMA, BUT somehow along the way, I became sidetracked. I was always the go-to babysitter in the neighborhood and loved working with kids when I was young. But when I came out as a lesbian in my twenties, I just assumed that meant I wouldn't become a mother, or if I did, that it would be through adoption. Coming of age in the eighties and nineties, and being wrapped up in the feminism of the Riot Grrrl Movement, a part of me also thought that being a mother didn't fit into the feminist ideal.

During that era, most of my friends were musicians, artists, or writers, and we were doing our best to distance ourselves from our parents, the Reagan politics, and the conservative mood that dominated the eighties. When I thought of parents, I thought of my own, and clearly I was not going to turn out like them. In my circle, I didn't know anyone who had children—we were childless and free. I simply couldn't comprehend how family and feminism could intersect. We were "Fighting for our Rights!" and trying to define ourselves as feminists. Somehow, the status quo of choosing motherhood seemed to support The Patriarchy rather than subvert it. I was aiming for subversion.

If my twenties were defined by politics, 'zines and riot grrrl rock shows, my thirties were defined by work and career. I became a workaholic, and my career was my baby. I was walking down the path of what I thought was the Perfect Feminist Lesbian: active in politics, hyper-career driven, unmarried, and childless. I threw myself into my work—it defined me. As a freelancer, I was on a high when I had a job, but depressed when I was out of work. Spiritually and emotionally, I was empty.

Then everything turned upside down: I met my partner, we fell in love, got married (yes, legally, during that small window in California), and decided we wanted a family. Was it possible? Could I be a wife and mother, even though I was gay? After taking a trip to Europe with my partner, the desire to be a mother started to creep in. I'll be honest, I'm not sure what it was about the trip to Europe that woke up my maternal desire. Perhaps by exploring another culture I had also rediscovered some lost landscape in myself. Maybe I wanted to expand on the happiness I had with my partner, to share the wonders of the world with a child—a family. Or perhaps the travel itself made me appreciate home and triggered my deep-seated nesting desires for a family. The Europe trip marked our one-year wedding anniversary, and four years together. I suppose that milestone also signified that we were ready to start a family, to share our amazing life with another. Whatever it was, it was like I remembered some past life . . . a former version of myself that wanted to be a mother and love a child unconditionally.

So my partner and I returned home and began the process of creating a family. We planned, conceived, and bore a daughter out of love. While I knew that raising a child in an unconventional family would be challenging, and that I'd be navigating landscapes that might not always be open and accepting, I never thought this journey would lead me to question my *own* identity.

As the birth mother of our daughter, Beatrice, I naturally fell into the role of the primary caregiver. I breastfed and wore our daughter from morning until night, and I was the one she slept with every night. It was for ease of breastfeeding, yes, but I also couldn't bear the thought of putting my precious newborn in a crib down the hall. I was in love with my new baby, and I was also completely surprised by how much I was in love with being a mama.

The minute she was in my arms, I knew I wasn't going back to work—ever—if I could help it. I wanted to be a stay-at-home mom, but what does that look like for a Feminist Lesbian? I looked everywhere for guidance and inspiration. I read the mommy blogs, pinned on Pinterest, and joined a variety of online community groups. I wanted to be "that" stay-at-home mom: you know, the one who was supported by her partner, kept a clean house, and created fresh, organic meals for our family. I fell for it—hook, line, and sinker.

I was active in the mommy blogosphere and on the advice boards. I could relate! I was just like those other (straight) mamas who struggled with breastfeeding, admonished our partners for not doing the dishes, and loved being mamas so much we happily gave up our careers for our children. I quickly fell into the "Crunchy Mama" segment of the online community: I practiced Attachment Parenting, used cloth diapers, breastfed exclusively, went to yoga, and only ate organic.

However, I quickly learned that a large segment of the "Crunchy Mamas" were not only straight (of course), but also devout Christians. So many bloggers were even (*gasp!*) Mormon. Mormons are the ones who hate gays, right? The ones who spent so much money trying to keep me from getting married? Jeez, what on earth would they do with a Lesbian Mama?

Perusing the online cloth-diaper swaps, I felt punched in the gut every time I saw "I love Jesus" avatars and scripture signatures (photos and identity descriptors associated with the online account names for my fellow "Crunchy Mamas"). Even my preference for cloth diapering was soiled by a healthy dose of judgment. I didn't know how to live in their world, one that I perceived as being based on a judgmental, righteous, oppressive, patriarchal construct. Sheltered in my own liberal bubble, I didn't know what to do. And worse, I began to doubt myself.

Thus, I hid who I was from my online acquaintances, and basically went back in the closet. When posting on the boards for advice about everything from car seats to colic, I always said "partner," but never used a pronoun, I LOL'ed along with the other ladies when they talked about their husbands, and I fit right in. I was living a lie. No, I never told anyone I was straight, but I never said otherwise, and to me, a lie of omission was just as bad.

Online identities are easy to create and obfuscate. *Wife, Crunchy Mama, DIY'er, loves Vintage Clothes.* Yeah, that's me, but an amended version. My avatar photo was a photo of my daughter and me from our cover on *Gay Parent* magazine—with my partner cropped out. Our family was on the cover of *Gay Parent* magazine! What happened to being out and proud? I marched in Dyke Marches in the nineties for visibility and rights. Who was I becoming?

It was easy to be vague on an advice board, or when running a simple diaper transaction. When a person is spending money on PayPal, it's immaterial whether my daughter has another mother instead of a father. No one can judge me. No one can ask me pointed questions.

But then I got one. I got one of *those* questions—one that forced me to open up and share the entirety of my identity.

Baby-wearing had become somewhat of an obsession for me, and I decided to have a custom carrier made to tote my daughter around at the farmer's markets while I bought my organic veggies. Good mama, right? I sought out a lovely stay-at-home mama who made wrap conversions. Send her a woven wrap and she transforms it into a Mei Tai carrier. We began a lovely email exchange. I live in Los

Angeles, she's from Los Angeles. We both cloth diaper ("I love hemp inserts! They are so absorbent!") and we both use amber necklaces on our DD's ("Darling Daughters" in Mommy Board lingo). We have so much in common! We exchanged photos of our little ones . . . and then I received a reply that came with the million dollar question:

"Your baby is so cute! Does she look like your husband?"

Do I tell her? *Well, actually, she looks like our donor, who happens to be my partner's brother.* I could just imagine the look on her face as she tried to process that one.

She was upfront and honest about her identity and her beliefs. A brief look on her "About me" page on her website and there it was: "Jesus Loving . . ." Having experienced the intense homophobia surrounding the Prop 8 initiative in California, to me that read: "Gays Hating . . ."

Why do I care what these women on the Internet think? In real life, I almost relish in outing myself. I look for opportunities to correct people's assumptions: "Your daughter plays drums! Does your husband play drums?" "No, my wife does. She got her a drum kit when she was just eighteen months old!" A smile changes to confusion (knitted eyebrows) to realization ("Oh, she's a *lesbian* . . .") to either complete acceptance or irritation. Somehow *seeing* the changes on people's faces as I tell them that my daughter has two moms is somewhat satisfying to me.

I almost typed back, "Yes, she looks like my partner," and hit send. But then I stopped.

What message was I sending my daughter? Be true to yourself (except when you are online and fear judgment, so you remain anonymous). Always accept others for who they are (except yourself, if you don't think you'll fit in—or others, if they are religious). Although my daughter was just an infant, I didn't want to start that pattern of hypocrisy and dishonesty.

By withholding information and assuming that I would be judged—*I* was the one doing the judging. I was the one not practicing acceptance and assuming that these other, religious mothers would not be accepting of me. It brought me to a whole new level of acceptance, for others and for myself.

Who am I to assume that someone's religious beliefs automatically dictate how they will feel about our family? It's a two-way street; I can't expect others to be open and accepting of me if I'm not willing to extend the same courtesy.

So I did it. I outed myself to this woman I had never met, but somehow cared so much about what she thought. Did she represent society's view of me? Would her acceptance of my lifestyle somehow validate it?

"No, my daughter looks a lot like me, and a lot like my partner. My partner's brother was our donor . . ."

I don't even remember what she said, I don't even remember if she replied or acknowledged what I said to her. I never saw the look on her face go from the knitted brows of confusion to the tight lips of a frown that I know so well. I never saw her face register, "Oh, she's a lesbian. A lesbian *mother.*" I know we exchanged a few more emails and she made me a gorgeous carrier that I use every week to carry my daughter on my back while I pick out organic Fuji apples at the local farmers market.

Acceptance is really the key to peace for me along this motherhood journey. I accept that I'm a crunchy, work at home, Attachment Parenting, Feminist Lesbian mother. And I accept that not everyone out there is okay with that. Once I acknowledged this, I started "outing" myself more on the "Crunchy Mama" boards. I also started posting less and less on the boards and started seeking out like-minded mamas in real life, mamas I could sit down and have coffee with, and actually see the smiles on their faces while we watched our kids play. The forums are still a great resource for practical information, but I stopped caring whether that mama in Indiana thought I was a bad parent because I chose to create a family with another woman. What other people think of me really doesn't matter. What my daughter thinks of me does.

As long as I'm true to myself and teach my daughter acceptance and love, I know I'm doing the best I can. And I'm creating an amazing life for my daughter and our family. Someone told me once that every family creates its own story, and when it comes to LGBT families, that's even more profound. Our daughter was planned, conceived, and born in love, and we are raising our family and creating our story with the hopes that our daughter will embrace and accept what we have created for her.

Now as I post on boards and chat with other mamas, I own my avatar: A smiling photo of a loving family with two moms—our cover story photo from *Gay Parent* magazine.

WHEN GOOD MOTHERS COME FROM BAD ONES /
GINA **CROSLEY-CORCORAN**

I NEVER WANTED CHILDREN. Based on my experiences growing up, I truly believed that all mothers hated their kids and that pregnancies were an ugly punishment bestowed upon any woman stupid enough to get caught without a condom. I speculated that every woman who had ever had a baby had merely done so to trap whatever man she was with at the time. It never occurred to me that a person would have a baby on purpose. The women around me certainly never seemed to.

You can understand, then, my reaction to news reports of kidnappings, where distraught mothers and fathers pleaded for the safe return of their child on the evening news. As a child, I honestly could not understand why the parents seemed so distressed. I thought to myself, *Aren't they glad to be rid of the kid? Don't all parents hate their offspring?*

Who were these mothers? Were they faking it for the cameras? My own mother appeared to have nothing in common with them, and neither did I, it seemed. I believed that I had no chance of being that breed of caring, concerned mother that I saw tearfully longing for her missing child. It was a given that I would fail at motherhood, so I never wanted to try. Not on purpose, anyway.

Growing up, my family environment was anything but functional. I was born to teen parents—my father was only fourteen years old, and my mother just seventeen. My father, barely pubescent and without so much as a driver's license to visit me when he wanted, was not expected to step up and take care of his baby. My mother simply did not want to.

My parents broke up while my mother was still pregnant, so my father wasn't around to help. Once I was born, my mother left it up to my fourteen-year-old aunt and grandparents to look after me. She would not even get out of bed to feed me. She forced my young aunt to tend to my feedings and diaper changes and to babysit me while she continued enjoying her teenage years. My mother paraded me around when it was convenient, but she had a habit of leaving me places when she got bored. My grandmother would often receive calls from relatives and friends asking her to come pick me up because my mother had deposited me somewhere before taking off again.

At some point, it was decided that my maternal grandparents would raise me. I became like their daughter, and I referred to them collectively as my parents. My mother, now eighteen and living with the man who became my stepfather, no longer took part in raising me. It was for the best. My mother was a violent person who treated me as a nuisance and beat me whenever I got in her way. When I was four years old, she stabbed my stepfather in the stomach with a paring knife right in front of me. He survived with a five-inch scar across his navel, but somehow, my mother wasn't charged and the whole incident was swept under the rug.

There was no formal adoption, but my grandparents were not formal people. They were poor, uneducated, and constantly on the move. There were periods of time, however, where my grandparents and I lived with my mother for a few weeks or months because *she* had an apartment and we were homeless. But even then, I still was not regarded as my mother's responsibility. When it was time for my grandparents to pick up and leave, there was no question that I would be going with them. Often, we left because my mother started a new cycle of physically and verbally abusing me. She was acting out what she had learned. Her father—my grandfather—physically abused me as well, but he didn't like it when my mother did it. Perhaps he did not like to have his own behavior mirrored back at him through his daughter.

It wasn't until my freshman year of high school, when I went to live with my aunt, that any sort of formal court hearing regarding my living arrangements took place. Since the school district required my aunt to have guardianship of me in order to enroll, my mother signed the papers and officially named my aunt as my legal guardian. It only made sense. My aunt had been like a mother to me since birth, and she was the only person in the family who yearned to provide a stable household for me. Not only was she my aunt, but she felt like my mother, my sister, and my friend. Unfortunately, she had her own problems. After ten years of suffering at the hands of a physically abusive husband, she finally divorced my uncle just six months after I moved in. He left us with the mobile home, and we suddenly found ourselves trying to survive on just the few dollars per hour she made working at the small-town grocery store.

During my sophomore year of school, my aunt could not afford to have the heat turned on. We spent a frigid Illinois winter burning old boxes in the fireplace to keep warm. During that same period, while visiting my mother, we were in a major car accident and my hand was injured. When my money from the insurance settlement came, my mother forced me to write my check over to her. I cried and begged her to give my aunt enough money from the settlement to get our heat turned on. She reluctantly agreed, handing over just a tiny fraction of what the insurance company had sent me, all the while berating me for wanting anything at all. Meanwhile, my aunt still could not afford to feed me, so most days I went without breakfast and lunch.

Around that time, my mother taught me how to smoke pot out of a bowl. I had no real interest in getting high with my mother, but being invited into her bedroom to do drugs was the only time I ever remember her giving me any attention. I wanted so badly for her to like me, and saw getting high as a way to bond with her. I did it because I thought she would think I was cool. For the few minutes I spent toking a bowl on her bed, I felt like she actually cared about me.

By my junior year of high school, I was back to living with my grandparents while my mother had moved her family to Florida, hoping to escape creditors. Though I was taller than my grandfather at this point, he still couldn't stop the habit of beating me when I upset him. Late one night, after coming home exhausted from working a second shift, with homework left to do for the next morning, my grandfather ordered me to the store for popcorn. I was tired and wasn't thinking straight. I came back with the wrong kind of popcorn, so he held me over the stove and punched me in the face repeatedly until I escaped to call the police. I couldn't think of anything else to do after that, so I ran away to my mother's new home in Florida, unable to anticipate how badly that would turn out.

After just a few months of living with her, my mother began abusing me again. I ran away to live with a cousin and her boyfriend, but my mother had me picked up by the police and dragged home. Within a few hours, neighbors were phoning police while my mother held me on the ground in front of her home in broad daylight, kicking me in the face. When the case worker arrived, I was taken to a half-way house for troubled youths. Within a few days, my remorseful grandparents had me on a plane back home to Illinois.

As I moved through puberty and into my sexually active teens, my lack of parenting role models became a form of birth control in itself. I learned all I needed to know about the pitfalls of motherhood by the way my own mother rejected the job. Once, she even told me in front of mixed company, "You are the abortion I should have had."

In stark contrast to the ever-deteriorating relationship I had with my mother, my father and I became close around the time that I graduated high school. He was in his early thirties by then and a bit more stable in his own life. He helped me buy a car and we started seeing more of each other. My dad knew he couldn't turn back the clock on the years he missed, so he committed himself to being a part of my life moving forward. We developed a strong relationship and tried to heal the effects of his eighteen-year absence from my life.

I arrived at adulthood saddled with the excessive emotional baggage of a stressful childhood, but I told myself that my destiny was mine to make. I forced myself to believe that anything that had ever been done to me was now a thing of the past and had no bearing on what kind of person I could become. I sold myself this lie for years, until one day I began experiencing unexplained panic attacks. I began seeing a therapist who asked me to sort out my experiences as a child. I tried calling my mother, hoping to see if she could explain to me why she treated me the way she did. She denied it all, and to hear her talk, she was Mother of the Year. The abuse, the abandonment, my damaged psyche—it meant nothing to her. There was no remorse.

A few short years later, I found myself in love with a man who wanted to marry me. He dreamed of being a parent, but I told him in no uncertain terms that I wasn't cut out for that job. Motherhood seemed like a one-way ticket to a life of regret and disappointment. I had no business burdening a child with my inherited parental failings. What had been done to me didn't need to be done to anyone else. My fiancé understood my misgivings about motherhood and agreed to take children off the table.

And then I got pregnant.

My knee-jerk reaction was to terminate the pregnancy. I felt terrified I'd continue the cycle of abuse. But I was not my mother. My pregnancy was not intentional, but the father of my baby was someone I loved deeply. He knew my history and he'd even met—and survived—my mother and grandparents. He believed in me and he believed in my capacity to be a loving mother. With his faith bolstering me, I decided to continue the pregnancy, and tentatively, I began to look forward to mothering.

But just before the wedding, my mother found one last way to break me down. We planned our wedding as an intimate affair, one that my mother was not invited to. When she got wind of my plans to exclude her, she wrote me several angry emails saying she wished I had never been born. She insisted that my father's family never loved me and had wanted her to abort me. She shared details of how my father's family had raised money for the procedure, and how she was sorry that she had not gone through with it. I was twelve weeks into my own pregnancy when she unleashed that bombshell on me.

After that day, I never spoke to my mother again. I spent my pregnancy wondering how I could possibly be a healthy, stable mother to a child when I had no examples to draw from. I resented the fetus inside me and often told my husband that he should probably raise the baby without me. I didn't believe I could pull it together for our child.

But then I gave birth and heard my baby cry for the first time. My world was instantaneously shattered and reborn anew. Any doubt that I could love my baby was erased on contact. As soon as I laid eyes on him, I knew that I wanted to spend my life being his mom. I could not believe how lucky I was to be given this person to love and cherish. I finally understood why parents would be distraught if their child went missing. It was nothing less than an epiphany: normal parents *do* love their children, not hate them.

Once I wrapped my arms around my son, I could not imagine letting him go. He was bound to my very soul and I could not fathom treating him the way my mother treated me. As I stared at him while he slept, I told myself I would never let him feel unloved or unsafe.

Now, seven years and three children later, I'm still unable to understand how or why my mother denied love and affection to her child. When I nurse my daughter to sleep, kissing the top of her head and pulling her heart closer to mine, I feel the pain of my own childhood all over again. When I cuddle with my children, my heart breaks to think about how my mother never cuddled with me. When I drag myself out of bed in the middle of the night to tend to a child's cries, it pains me to think about the way my mother refused to respond to my cries. My mother never rocked me against her breast in the wee hours of the morning. She deprived me of that love; a love that no one else in the world can ever offer me.

So every day, I strive to do better than she did. I am battling my own demons and I am not a perfect mother. Sometimes I yell. Sometimes I don't listen. Sometimes I catch myself saying or doing things that my own mother did. But I consistently work to be the mother that my children deserve. I have broken the cycle of abuse. I never thought it was possible, but sometimes even a bad mother can produce a good one.

GIVE ME MY 'A' IN SCARLET /
TARA JEAN BERNIER

Yeah, thank you for that blank stare,
that one you gave when you realized
what you let go from your mouth.
Oh yes, that was ignorance defined.

You ask, "How do you do it,
don't you miss them when they're away from you?
I couldn't do it."

Miss my sons? But it's only been two hours
since I've seen them last.
Who is taking care of them?
Their father.

"Oh, but daddies just don't
do it like mommies do."

Look—the mama wars are absolutely
the best way to sell a magazine.
Sure, pop a kid who looks older than three
on a disembodied tit, and make it glossy for *Newsweek*
and the world will break. The fuck. Down.

Or, tell women they can't have it all.
Put it on the cover of the *Atlantic*
and watch every morning talk show come up
with a new guilt-inducing headline. Yes, they sell magazines by stoking
the fires of the Mommy Wars.

And okay, I'll be honest,
I love a good fight—but Bitch,
you're not worth my time.

Yes, I am mother of two—
mother of two sons—
mother of two sons, aged five and three—
named Kai and Keegan.
Mother of two.

And yes, I work full-time,
and advise four clubs,
and stay late after school,
and, why yes,
I am on the board of that nonprofit.

And yes, I go out a couple of times a week.
Yes, without my husband.

Yes, at night.
Yes, sometimes I drink.

Shall I dig that Scarlet 'A' out of my pocket?
Or do you keep one on hand,
for women like me?

No, you're right—
I'm not home to pick them up from school.
Their sitter picks them up.
But yeah, she's better at hide-and-seek than I am.

No, I didn't can/preserve/freeze this year's
garden's organic, vitamin-rich kale,
you Happy Valley guru.
I did, though, make a boozy, rum-peach jam
that makes everyone drool.

See the cookies,
I bake long into the night,
we will eat those for breakfast on Saturday mornings,
while we watch *Power Rangers*.
And speaking of sacrifice—
Who writes this shit?

And have you met my boys?
Ages three and five?
You know what they like best about me?
That the characters in their books that I read
have voices better than their favorite cartoons on TV.

They love that they
are never afraid of the dark,

because I know where to buy all the zombie-proof roofing and siding.

And when my son, aged three, asked,
"Could you teach me how to be a superhero?"
And I replied, "I'm not sure I know all the rules."
My son aged five jumped in to say,
"Yeah you do, Mama—don't you remember?"
"How would I remember, Kai?"
"Silly mama—Because you are one."

See, the Mommy Wars are bullshit,
because we all just love differently.
I love with super powers.
Super powers fueled by a sweet case of ADHD,
and a twelve-pack of Magic Hat.

My cape is made from the possibility
I want to show my boys,
from the worlds they should
grow to explore.

And you know what?
Hand over that 'A'
because it stands for
Awesome, or Amazing,
or Able, or Absolutely cooler than you.

Oh right, I wasn't going to engage
in this Mommy War.

Because I am mother of two,
mother of two boys,
mother of two boys, ages five and three.

Mother of two boys,
who never stop,
who tell knock-knock jokes,
who drive their mother to drink,
just a little bit.

And as that mother,
I would swallow hot coals
to make sure they were all right.

Mother of two boys, aged five and three,
named Kai and Keegan,
carved out of my heart.
Mother of two.

ABOUT THE CONTRIBUTORS

PAULINE ABRAHAM is the pseudonym of an author and editor living in the Pacific Northwest.

Writer and activist **JENNIFER BAUMGARDNER** is the author of *Look Both Ways: Bisexual Politics, Abortion & Life, F 'em!: Goo Goo, Gaga, and Some Thoughts on Balls,* as well co-author of the Third Wave classics *Manifesta: Young Women, Feminism, and the Future* and *Grassroots: A Field Guide to Feminist Activism.* She owns Soapbox, Inc., a feminist speaker's bureau that runs Feminist Summer Camps in New York City. She writes for *Glamour, The New York Times, The Nation, Real Simple, Harper's Bazaar,* and *Babble,* among other outlets, and has made two award-winning documentaries: *I Had an Abortion* (2005) and *It Was Rape* (2013). Originally from Fargo, ND, she lives in Manhattan with her husband, two sons, and an Abyssinian named Bikini.

TARA JEAN BERNIER didn't know she could write poetry till she started writing poetry. Crushed by a nasty case of PPD after the birth of her second son, she began blogging every day at happyvalleymama.com as a form of therapy. Currently she is an English teacher at one of the ten oldest high schools in America, where she teaches writing, literature, and the occasional feminist manifesto, all with a good dose of humor. Mama to Kai and Keegan, she has called the Happy Valley of Western Massachusetts her home for the last ten years.

SARAH WERTHAN BUTTENWIESER is a freelance writer based in Northampton, Massachusetts, whose work has appeared in *The New York Times, Brain Child Magazine,* and *Salon,* amongst others. Follow her on twitter: @standshadows.

T. F. CHARLTON is the founder and editor of Are Women Human?, a space for queer feminist and critical race analysis of religion, media, and pop culture. As a freelance writer, she has contributed to *The Guardian, Salon, Religion Dispatches,* EBONY.com, and more.

SORAYA CHEMALY is a cultural critic and feminist activist who writes and talks about the role of gender in politics, religion, and media. She is a regular contributor to *The Huffington Post, RH Reality Check, Fem2.0, Role/Reboot, BitchFlicks,* and *Alternet.* Soraya makes frequent media appearances as a commenter in discussions of these topics, including as a guest on NPR's *Talk of the Nation,* Sirius XM progressive radio, *Voice of Russia* and *The Huffington Post's* regular *HuffPost Live* roundtable news programs.

GINA CROSLEY-CORCORAN, CD(DONA), CCCE, is a former-rocker-chick-turned-mom, a blogger, and a busy doula. She's also a passionate advocate for women's reproductive rights and is currently working on a Master of Public Health in Maternal Child Health. At home, she's a mother of three spirited children and wife to a bilingual middle school teacher who laughs at all her jokes.

ELIZABETH CROSSEN grew up in central Pennsylvania and is a recent graduate of Penn State University with concentrations in Sociology and Women's Studies, and African American Studies. She lives in Philadelphia, currently serving as an AmeriCorps VISTA, after which she will be heading to graduate school. Her work has been published several times in Penn State's liberal arts publication, *Agora*. She has presented various papers at the Social Thought Conference, the Women's Studies Graduate Organization conference, the National Women's Studies conference, and the New York African Studies Association conference. Crossen is a single mother to two fantastic little boys.

ARWYN DAEMYIR, creator of the blog Raising My Boychick, is a massage therapist, writer, mental illness survivor, and mother living in the Pacific Northwest. Her words have appeared in venues such as *Bitch* magazine, NPR.org, *Hoax Zine*, *Global Comment*, and university courses in two hemispheres. Her blog has nothing to do with her chickens, but don't try to tell them that.

K. J. DELL'ANTONIA (@KJDellAntonia) writes and edits the Motherlode blog for *The New York Times*. She is the co-author of *Reading with Babies, Toddlers and Twos* (Sourcebooks 2013). Her work has also appeared on *Slate*.com's DoubleX and its XXFactor blog, on Babble.com, and in *Parents*, *Parenting*, *Kiwi*, and the still-regretted *Wondertime* (and other publications). She lives in New Hampshire with her husband and an assortment of kids and animals.

SHANNON DRURY is a Minneapolis-based writer, at-home parent, and feminist activist. Her writing has appeared in *Bitch* magazine, *HipMama*, *Skirt!*, and many Twin Cities publications. Her blog, The

Radical Housewife, was named a Top Political Mom Blog by Circle of Moms Online and was named one of "30 Political Mom Bloggers Who Will Change Your Vote" by website The Stir. In 2012, she completed her sixth term as president of the Minnesota chapter of NOW. Her political memoir, *The Radical Housewife,* will be published by Medusa's Muse Press in 2013.

LISA DUGGAN is a writer and editor, and the owner of American Woman Publishing LLC, a media company dedicated to serving contemporary families which produces *The Modern Village: Continuing Education for Parents* and *The Parent du Jour.* Lisa's writing can be found at TheMotherHoodBlog.com and *Forbes,* and she can be found on Twitter @motherhoodmag.

AMBER DUSICK is the illustrator and author of the bestselling humor book *Parenting: Illustrated with Crappy Pictures* (Harlequin Nonfiction). Her blog at CrappyPictures.com attracts over a million visits per month. She lives in Los Angeles with her two boys, a husband, and two black cats. She also has a fish, but usually leaves him out of bios.

ANDIE FOX writes about motherhood from feminist, political, and personal perspectives. She is the author of the popular blog, blue milk, which has been the recipient of multiple honors and was recently featured in *Ms.* magazine. Fox is also a contributing author to the anthology, *The 21st Century Motherhood Movement.* Her writing has appeared on various blogs, including Moms Rising, and she has presented at conferences on motherhood, work and family, feminism, and social media. Fox has written for *The Guardian, Daily Life,* and also Melbourne's *The Wheeler Centre.* She is sometimes heard on Australia's ABC radio.

LIZ HENRY is an award-winning writer and the hell-raising voice behind the website, *The Lizzness.* She graduated from Arcadia University with a degree in English literature. Henry lives with her family in Atlanta, but was made in Philadelphia. Read more of her writing at lizzness.com

HEATHER HEWETT is a writer, a professor, and a mother. She has published essays, reviews, and articles in a range of publications, including *The Washington Post; The Women's Review of Books;* CNN. com; *The Christian Science Monitor; Brain, Child: The Magazine for Thinking Mothers;* and anthologies such as *A Slant of Light: Contemporary Women Writers of the Hudson Valley* (Codhill Press). An associate professor of English and Women's, Gender, and Sexuality Studies at the State University of New York at New Paltz, she teaches courses on literature, women's studies, and nonfiction writing. Born and bred in Oklahoma, she lives in the lower Hudson Valley with her family.

STEPHANIE KALOI is the managing editor of Offbeat Families, a freelance writer for xoJane.com, and a wedding photographer. She enthusiastically lives in Portland, OR, with her husband, son, and adopted mongrel of a dog while juggling a zillion projects and nerding out to *Star Wars* on the regular.

JOY LADIN is a David and Ruth Gottesman Professor of English at Stern College for Women of Yeshiva University, and is the parent of three children, ages 8 to 18. She is the author of the newly published memoir, *Through the Door of Life: A Jewish Journey Between Genders,* and six books of poetry: *Coming to Life* (Forward Fives award winner); *Transmigration* (Lambda Literary Award finalist); *Psalms; The Book of Anna;* and *Alternatives to History.* She has received a Fulbright Scholarship as well as a fellowship from the American Council of Literary Societies.

SHARON LERNER is a journalist focusing on work-life balance, education, health equity, and other issues affecting families in the

United States. She's a senior fellow at Demos, and the author of *The War on Moms: On Life in a Family-Unfriendly Nation* (Wiley, 2010), which NPR called, "A stinging account of how public policy and private businesses have failed to adapt to working mothers." Lerner has covered a wide range of stories in her work as a writer, reporter, and public radio producer, though this is her first piece about disgust.

ANNE-MARIE LINDSEY is the author of the popular personal blog, Do Not Faint, as well as the blog of the same name for *Psychology Today*. She also guest posts at parenting blog Fit for Moms, the blog for baby carrier company Onya Baby, and the Feminist Breeder Resource site. Anne-Marie's writing is driven by her desire to chronicle her journey through planning a pregnancy, pregnancy itself, and motherhood in the face of a life-long struggle with severe anxiety and depression. She hopes to write a memoir to reach even more women who have struggled with the same difficult choices.

ERIKA LUST is an independent erotic filmmaker, author, and founder of Erika Lust Films. After graduating from Lund University with a degree in Political Science and Feminism, Lust moved to Barcelona, where her production company was established in 2005. She has directed four award-winning erotic films: *Five Hot Stories for Her*, *Barcelona Sex Project*, *Life Love Lust*, and *Cabaret Desire*, as well as some shorts, and is currently working on her fifth. Her written works include *Good Porn: a Woman's Guide*, *The Erotic Bible to Europe*, *Love Me Like You Hate Me*, and *La Canción de Nora*. Lust is committed to forging a new concept of sexual expression within the adult film industry, with the inclusion of women's voices, fresh aesthetics, and a humanistic approach to sex. Learn more at erikalust.com

KIMBERLY MORAND resides in Canada with her lively four-year-old son and her handsome husband of ten years. In her pre-baby days, she worked as a registered nurse on a pediatric emergency department.

In between folding laundry and waging war against the neverending accumulation of dog hair on the floor, she writes the personal blog called All Work and No Play Makes Mommy Go Something Something. She is a four-year postpartum depression and postpartum anxiety survivor.

CARLA NAUMBURG, PhD, is a mother of two daughters, a clinical social worker, and a writer. She is a contributing editor for Kveller.com, the mindful parenting blogger for PsychCentral.com, and her work has appeared in a number of academic journals and online publications. She lives with her family outside of Boston, Massachusetts.

NERISSA NIELDS has been a member of the band The Nields since 1991. She has toured North America, been on major labels, played to tens of thousands from stages all across the continent, and has passionate fans all over the world. Nerissa published her first novel, *Plastic Angel* (Scholastic Press) in 2005. She is also the author of *How to Be an Adult: A Musician's Guide to Navigating One's 20s* (Leveller's Press/Mercy House 2008 and 2013). She wrote *All Together Singing in the Kitchen: The Musical Family* (Shambhala, 2011) with her sister Katryna. She is currently working on her second novel, *The Big Idea*, the story of a rock band who is also a family. Nerissa also maintains three blogs: May Day Café, Singing in the Kitchen, and How to Be an Adult. Trained as a life coach by Martha Beck, Nerissa runs writing workshops and retreats out of her home in Northampton, Massachusetts, where she lives with her husband and children. For more information, visit www. nerissanields.com

KRISTEN OGANOWSKI is a writer, birth doula, maternity care advocate, PhD candidate in philosophy, and mother of three from Columbus, Ohio. Her blog, Birthing Beautiful Ideas, explores issues in pregnancy, birth, motherhood, and feminism. In 2011, Babble.com designated Birthing Beautiful Ideas as one of Top 50 Pregnancy Blogs, naming Kristen the

#1 overall friendliest expert. In addition to friendly expertise, Kristen is passionate about making issues like informed decision-making in maternity care and feminist approaches to parenting as accessible as possible.

VICTORIA BROOKE RODRIGUES is a Deep-South-raised poet, essayist, and librarian. The ocean is her home parish and reggae is her Gospel music. She shares this life with her husband, two sons, and their dogs, chickens, and fish, in Albuquerque, New Mexico.

ABBY SHER is a writer and performer living in Brooklyn, New York. Her memoir, *Amen, Amen, Amen: Memoir of a Girl Who Couldn't Stop Praying* was published by Scribner in October 2009. It got a nod from *Oprah* and won *ELLE* Readers' Prize, *Chicago Tribune's* Best of 2009, and *Moment Magazine's* Emerging Writers Award. Abby also wrote a young adult book, *Kissing Snowflakes* for Scholastic in 2007. Abby writes for *The New York Times, The L.A. Times, Self, Jane, Elle, Elle UK, Marie Claire, HeeB, Redbook,* and is a regular contributor for *Psychology Today*. Before moving to New York, Abby wrote and performed for The Second City and ImprovOlympic. Today, she is working on a nonfiction book about sex trafficking (serious) and a TV show about ugly parents (silly). She also performs at different theaters in New York and narrates audiobooks for kids.

NAOMI SHULMAN has written essays and articles for *The New York Times, Real Simple, Ladies' Home Journal,* and *Yankee,* among others. A former staffer at *Wondertime,* the late Disney-owned parenting magazine, she wrote for both the magazine and the staff blog, and was also a regular contributor at AOL's SlashFood and KitchenDaily. She lives in Northampton, MA, with her husband and two daughters, and is at work on a novel.

DEBORAH SIEGEL, PhD is an expert on gender, politics, and the unfinished business of feminism across generations. She is the author of *Sisterhood, Interrupted: From Radical Women to Grrls Gone Wild* (Palgrave), coeditor of the literary anthology *Only Child* (Harmony/ Random House), founder of the group blog Girl w/ Pen housed at The Society Pages, and cofounder of both the webjournal The Scholar & Feminist Online and the popular website She Writes. Deborah's writings on women, feminism, contemporary families, sex, and popular culture have appeared in venues including CNN.com, *The Washington Post, The Guardian, The Forward, Slate's* The Big Money, *The Huffington Post, The American Prospect, Ms., More,* and has been featured on TV and radio, including *The Today Show, Good Morning America Radio,* and *The Wendy Williams Experience.* She is a Visiting Scholar in Gender and Sexuality Studies at Northwestern University and is working on a graphic memoir about the gendering of earliest childhood. She lives in Chicago with her husband and twins and lives online at www.deborahsiegelwrites.com

CHRISTINA SOLETTI is a mama, wife, producer, conservationist, DIY'er, vintage fanatic, dog lover, social media expert, and writer living in sunny Los Angeles with her partner Patty, daughter Beatrice, and their dogs. She is passionate about babies, baby-wearing, birth, yoga, natural living, and healthy eats. When not spending time with her sweet toddler girl, either outdoors or reading her a book, she's most likely blogging about all of the above on her blog, Steady Happy.

SHAY STEWART-BOULEY is the Executive Director of a faith-based, nonprofit community center focused on youth. In 2003, Shay started writing for publications such as the *Portland Press Herald* and the *Journal Tribune,* later that year landing her own column in the *Portland Phoenix.* In 2011, she won a New England Press Association Award for her work writing on diversity issues. Shay has also been blogging at her personal site, Black Girl in Maine since 2008, where she admits she is a mother but not a mommy blogger. She pontificates on social issues but isn't a social commentator *per se*, and she is a woman of color but not a race-issue blogger. Black Girl in Maine was named to Babble's Top 100 Mom Bloggers of 2011 and 2012.

SARAH EMILY TUTTLE-SINGER is an LA Expat (reluctantly) growing roots in Israel. She's learning to love being an outsider. After all, the view from the edge is exquisite. Fueled by a double-shot latte, she (over)shares her (mis)adventures across the Internet, including on Kveller.com, *Times of Israel, Jezebel,* and *Offbeat Mama.* She is dangerous when bored.

CHRISTY TURLINGTON BURNS is the founder of Every Mother Counts, a campaign to end preventable deaths caused by pregnancy and childbirth around the world. Every Mother Counts informs, engages, and mobilizes new audiences to take action to improve the health and well-being of girls and women worldwide. In 2010, Christy directed and produced *No Woman, No Cry,* a documentary film about the global state of maternal health. Prior to her work as a global maternal health advocate, Christy focused her activism on smoking prevention and cessation after losing her father to lung cancer in 1997. She collaborated on several public health service campaigns and launched an award-winning website, SmokingIsUgly.com in 2002. Christy is also an avid yogi and merged her love of the practice and writing to author her first book, *Living Yoga: Creating a Life Practice* (Hyperion 2002). She has contributed to *Marie Claire* magazine, *Yoga Journal* and *Teen Vogue,* along with contributions to *The Huffington Post,* BlogHer, MomsRising, Canada's *Globe and Mail* and the UK's *Evening Standard.*

JESSICA VALENTI—called one of the Top 100 Inspiring Women in the world by *The Guardian*—is the author of four books, including *Why Have Kids: A New Mom Explores the Truth About Parenting and Happiness.* She also is the editor of the anthology *Yes Means Yes: Visions of Female Sexual Power* and *A World without Rape,* which was named one of *Publishers Weekly*'s Top 100 Books of 2009. Jessica is the founder of Feministing.com, which *Columbia Journalism Review* calls "head and shoulders above almost any writing on women's issues in mainstream media." Her writing has appeared in *The Washington Post, The Nation, The Guardian (UK), The American Prospect, Ms.* magazine, *Salon* and *Bitch* magazine. She has appeared on *The Colbert Report* and *The Today Show,* among others, and was profiled in *The New York Times Magazine* under the headline "Fourth Wave Feminism."

CANDACE WALSH is the author of *Licking the Spoon: A Memoir of Food, Family, and Identity* (Seal Press, 2012), and co-editor of *Dear John, I Love Jane: Women Write About Leaving Men for Women,* a Lambda Literary Award Finalist, as well as the editor of *Ask Me About My Divorce: Women Open Up About Moving On* (both by Seal Press). She lives in Santa Fe with her wife, Laura André, and two children. Read more about her at candacewalsh.com, follow her on Twitter @ candacewalsh, and catch her blog posts at *The Huffington Post* and LickingtheSpoonBook.com

ALY WINDSOR is a mother, partner, news editor, and blogger at www.embracerelease.com. Exercise is her anxiolytic of choice, but gardening, oversharing online, and red wine also help.

ABOUT THE EDITOR

AVITAL NORMAN NATHMAN is a former teacher and lifelong learner turned freelance writer. Her work, which places a feminist lens on a variety of topics, including motherhood, gender, and reproductive rights, has been featured in *Bitch* magazine, *Bamboo Family* magazine, CNN, HLNtv.com, *RH Reality Check*, *Offbeat Mama*, *Kveller*, *The New York Times* Motherlode and more. In addition to her blog, The Mamafesto, Avital has a regular series, "The Femisphere," for *Ms.* magazine's website, as well as the feminist parenting column, "Mommie Dearest," for *The Frisky*. Based in Western Massachusetts with her husband and seven-year-old son, Avital also enjoys digging in her urban garden, hosting dance parties in her kitchen, and is on a constant hunt for the perfect cup of Chai.

ACKNOWLEDGMENTS

t's said that no one person writes a book—this is infinitely more accurate when it comes to an anthology. While the concept for this book stemmed from a combination of my dreams and frustrations, it certainly wouldn't have come to fruition without the help, work, and support of many wonderful people. It is with a full heart and immense gratitude that I acknowledge the following people who were all instrumental in their own way in helping get this book off the ground and onto the shelves:

To my Seal Press team, Krista Lyons and Laura Mazer— I could not have asked for a better introduction into the world of book publishing. Thank you. And this book certainly wouldn't be what it is without my fairy godmother of a development editor, Merrik Bush-Pirkle, whose comments, notes, and reassurance were crucial in allowing everything to come together.

Mary Ann Zimmerman and Amber Fatone, your combined

contract knowledge rivals any lawyer's, and I'm thankful you didn't laugh at what must have surely been the most random, ridiculous questions.

To my various sounding boards and hand holders: Rachael Berkey, Tope Charlton, Anne-Marie Lindsey, Nicole Linn, Emily McAvan, Carla Naumburg, Hannah Richards, Sarah Tuttle-Singer, the Writer's Anonymous gals, and my Jam Girlz. The encouragement and support I received from all of you was instrumental as I worked on this project.

I've been lucky to have examples of great parenting from the get-go. Thank you so much to both of my parents, Betty and Moshe Norman; my Bubby, Esther Sal; and my mother-in-law, Sharon Nathman, for providing me with the framework and inspiration to forge my own good mothering path.

Marc and Elijah—I wouldn't even be writing this without either of you. I couldn't have managed this without your support and cheerleading. "T.Hanks" for making this whole parenting thing one of the best and most interesting gigs around.

And to all the phenomenal women who contributed their words and stories to this book— you are all truly the definition of what it means to be a good mother. Thank you.

SELECTED TITLES FROM SEAL PRESS

For more than thirty years, Seal Press has published groundbreaking books. By women. For women.

Inconsolable: How I Threw My Mental Health out with the Diapers, by Marrit Ingman. $14.95, 978-1-58005-140-8. With candor and humor, Ingman paints a portrait of the darker side of parenthood—complete with stories of postpartum depression, sleepless nights, and playgroup drinking games.

I Love Mondays: And Other Confessions from Devoted Working Moms, by Michelle Cove. $16.00, 978-1-58005-435-5. Michelle Cove explores the common difficulties faced by working moms—and provides real-life anecdotes, helpful new perspectives, and mom-tested strategies for dealing with each one.

How to Fit a Car Seat on a Camel: And Other Misadventures Traveling with Kids, edited by Sarah Franklin. $15.95, 978-1-58005-242-9. This anthology of outrageous and funny stories captures the mayhem that accompanies traveling with children.

Confessions of a Naughty Mommy: How I Found My Lost Libido, by Heidi Raykeil. $14.95, 978-1-58005-157-6. The Naughty Mommy shares her bedroom woes and woo-hoos with other mamas who are rediscovering their sex lives after baby and are ready to think about it, talk about it, and DO it.

The Goodbye Year: Surviving Your Child's Senior Year in High School, by Toni Piccinini. $16.00, 978-1-58005-486-7. Part self-help, part therapy, and completely honest, this sensitive companion is for mothers facing the life-changing transition that occurs when children graduate from high school.

The Stay-at-Home Survival Guide: Field-Tested Strategies for Staying Smart, Sane, and Connected When You're Raising Kids at Home, by Melissa Stanton. $15.95, 978-1-58005-247-4. The essential how-to book for stay-at-home mothers, written by a media-savvy former "working mom".

Find Seal Press Online
www.SealPress.com
www.Facebook.com/SealPress
Twitter: @SealPress